FROM
Violence
TO
Wholeness

Ken Butigan
In Collaboration with Patricia Bruno, O.P.

Pace e Bene Franciscan Nonviolence Center

FROM
Violence
TO
Wholeness

*a ten part program
in the spirituality and practice of
active nonviolence*

Ken Butigan
In collaboration with Patricia Bruno, O.P.
Pace e Bene Franciscan Nonviolence Center

Pace e Bene (pronounced *pah-chay bay-nay*) means "peace and all good" in Italian. St. Francis of Assisi used this expression as a greeting and as a means of proclaiming the way of nonviolence in the midst of a violent world.

Pace e Bene Franciscan Nonviolence Center is located in Las Vegas, Nevada, with an office in Berkeley, California. The center offers resources to assist in the journey of personal and social transformation, such as retreats, workshops, presentations, classes and a variety of publications, including its quarterly newsletter, *The Wolf of Pace e Bene*.

Pace e Bene's staff and animating group engage in nonviolent action and work with a wide range of nonviolent movements for justice and peace.

We are available to lead the one-day *From Violence To Wholeness Workshop* and the one-day *From Violence To Wholeness Facilitator's Workshop* in local communities.

Las Vegas Office
1420 W. Bartlett Ave., Las Vegas, NV 89106
phone & fax: (702) 648-2281
website: www.paceebene.org; e-mail: fvtw@paceebene.org

Northern California Office
2398 Bancroft Way, Berkeley, CA 94704 phone:
(510) 649-3500 fax: (510) 649-3088
e-mail: pbcal@paceebene.org

We are grateful for the permission to use copyrighted materials from the following publishing companies and individuals:

Rosemary Lynch, O.S.F. and Alain Richard, O.F.M., "The Decalogue for a Spirituality of Nonviolence." Printed by permission of the authors.

John Dear, "Forgetting Who We Are," published in *Disarming the Heart: Toward a Vow of Nonviolence* (Paulist Press, 1987). Reprinted by permission of the author.

Nancy Schreck, "The Faithful Nonviolence of Jesus." Printed by permission of the author.

Peter Ediger, "Who Is Well Off? The Beatitudes of Jesus and the Attitides of a Domination System." Reprinted by permission of the author.

The Nonviolence Resource Centre in Argenta, British Columbia for use of K. Louise Schmidt's "Violence against Women and Children," from *To Live in Peace: A Handbook for the Heart — Nonviolent Approaches for Families and Communities* (1994). Reprinted by permission of the Nonviolence Resource Centre.

Shelley Douglass, "The Power of Noncooperation." Printed by permission of the author.

"How St. Francis Tamed the Very Fierce Wolf of Gubbio," *The Omnibus of Franciscan Sources.* Reprinted with permission from The Franciscan Herald Press.

Susannah Malarkey, O.P., "The Spirituality of Nonviolence and Reverence for the Earth." Printed by permission of the author.

Thomas Berry, "A Moment of Grace." Reprinted introduction to Martha Heyneman's *The Breathing Cathedral* (Sierra Club, 1993). Reprinted by permission of the author.

Cesar Chavez's "Letter from Delano." Copyright 1969 Christian Century Foundation. Reprinted by permission from the April 23, 1969 issue of the *Christian Century.*

Bill Moyer for "Strategic Assumptions of the Movement Action Plan" and "The Eight Stages of a Successful Social Movement," *The Practical Strategist,* Social Movement Empowerment Project, 1990. Reprinted by permission of the author.

Marie Dennis and Terence Miller, "The Violence of Economics." Reprinted by permission of the authors.

Martin Luther King, Jr., "A Way of Nonviolence," *Ground Zero,* Winter, 1992. Reprinted by permission of Ground Zero Center for Nonviolent Action.

Susan Kling, "Fannie Lou Hamer: Baptism by Fire." Reprinted from *Reweaving the Web of Life: Feminism and Nonviolence,* edited by Pam McAllister (New Society Publishers, 1982). Reprinted by permission of New Society Publishers.

Servicio Paz y Justicia, "Preparing for Nonviolence." Reprinted from *Relentless Persistence: Nonviolent Action in Latin America* (New Society Publishers, 1991), edited by Philip McManus and Gerald Schlabach. Reprinted by permission of New Society Publishers.

Bill Cane, "The Church Universal: Circles of Faith," *Circles of Hope: Breathing Life and Spirit into a Wounded World* (Orbis Books, 1992). Reprinted by permission of Orbis Books.

CONTENTS

Introduction

Healing Our Woundedness: The Transforming Power of Active Nonviolence

Introduction
Healing Our Woundedness:
The Transforming Power of Active Nonviolence

From Violence To Wholeness is a ten part study and action program that explores nonviolence as a creative, powerful and effective process for addressing and resolving the conflicts in our lives and in the life of the world. Drawing on the vision of Jesus, Gandhi, Martin Luther King, Jr., Shelley Douglass and many others, this program offers your church, community, or group resources to deepen the journey from fear to freedom, from despair to hope, from violence to wholeness.

Facing Violence

Whether we like it or not, most of us are enrolled in a class called "Violence 101."

This class is not confined to a particular setting or time of day. Nobody asks if we want to attend. We don't need letters of reference or a high grade point average. It is taught everywhere, open to all. Our teachers are the media, with their flow of violent images and messages, and our society's values of consumerism, rugged individualism and superiority. Sometimes we receive *extra* tutoring from our family and co-workers. We take *special* workshops when our country goes to war or when violence erupts in the streets. Consciously or not, we are continually being schooled in the logic and practice of emotional, verbal, physical or structural violence.

What do we learn in this class? First, we are taught that the world is a dangerous place and that human beings are intrinsically violent. This is especially true of our enemies, who are the *most* violent and are beyond redemption or change. Faced with these cold facts, we learn our second lesson: the only way to deal with violence is to accommodate it, avoid it, or use violence ourselves. Television, our families, and the policies of the government teach us these methods, which we then try out in real life. With every conflict, we rehearse these three "scripts" by going along with violence, by running from it, or by throwing a physical or verbal punch.

The great illusion of violence is that it will solve our problems decisively. Unfortunately, conflicts often do not end when violence is used; they generally continue to smolder or escalate.

Violence 101's ultimate lesson is that violence feeds on itself and cannot be extinguished; there is always residual resentment and injustice. What is our society's answer to this spiral of violence? *More violence.* From this point of view, being human means becoming chronically suspicious of a world populated with real and potential enemies where unresolved anger and hurt are forever mounting.

The world *can* be dangerous, *and* we face conflicts our whole lives. But are we condemned to an endless cycle of retaliation and domination? The traditional responses to violence often make matters worse because they fail to address root causes and they lose sight of the integrity of those in conflict. They are fundamentally unreliable and ineffective. They also keep us from seeing what violence truly is: *emotional, verbal or physical behavior that dominates, diminishes or destroys ourselves and others.*

Violence crosses boundaries without permission. Violence disrupts authentic relationships. Violence separates us from others. It defiles the human person and desecrates the image of God. It is a process of economic, racial, social or cultural domination. To become truly human and to faithfully worship the God of Love means challenging this violence. Transforming these patterns of destructiveness is a sacred journey from fear to freedom, from despair to hope, from violence to wholeness.

The Nonviolent Alternative

Jesus, Gandhi, Dorothy Day, Martin Luther King, Jr. and many others have declared with their lives an alternative to the treadmill of violence. They have preached and practiced active nonviolence as a way to resolve conflict humanely and effectively, to become genuinely human, and to be faithful to the Nonviolent God.

Woundedness lies at the roots of violence in ourselves, in others, and in our culture. Active nonviolence comes face to face with these wounds. This includes identifying and gradually transforming our personal and social "scripts" that keep us in the rut of violence. But even more profoundly, active nonviolence makes contact with *the sacredness that lies deeper than our wounds.* This sacredness is the presence of the God who longs for our wholeness. It is where our truest selves live, the depths where we receive the gift of our richness, our authenticity, and our capacity for compassion. It is the spiritual center where we come to our senses, recover our balance, and reclaim our humanity.

By facing our woundedness and acknowledging our sacredness, active nonviolence prepares us to address the conflicts we face in our lives and in the life of our world. We are able to see the woundedness and the sacredness of those with whom we struggle. We are able to:

○ Let go of our traditional scripts and allow our truest self to be fully present
○ Creatively interrupt the cycle of retaliatory violence
○ Acknowledge and safeguard the humanity of the opponent as well as our own
○ Identify and struggle nonviolently for an agreement that respects all parties.

From Violence To Wholeness: "Active Nonviolence 101"

From Violence To Wholeness is a ten-part study and action program that explores the spirituality and practice of active nonviolence. Produced by Pace e Bene Franciscan Nonviolence Center, *From Violence To Wholeness* offers a theological vision of nonviolence *and* a toolbox of techniques that we can use in our daily lives. Local churches, campus ministries, Catholic women's and men's religious congregations, and Pax Christi USA groups have used this series. Through presentations, small group reflections, scripture, readings, and keeping a nonviolence journal, participants explore how to use active nonviolence in their lives. The program explores how:

○ Nonviolence is an act of faith in the God of Love and Justice
○ Human beings are called to love and be loved
○ Reality is connection; we are called to transform all that divides human beings from themselves, from one another, and from the Earth
○ Active nonviolence is an effective way to break the spiral of retaliatory violence and to create options for a more humane world.

The Structure of the *From Violence To Wholeness* Program

There are many ways to enter the spiritual journey of nonviolent transformation. The following curriculum — ten sessions, two hours per session — is offered as a framework for exploring the spirituality and practice of active nonviolence. Each session generally includes:

○ *Opening prayer or meditation*
   Samples are provided — you may want to create your own.
○ *Reflections on personal issues or experiences that have arisen since the previous session*
○ *Small group reflection on our life experience*
○ *Discussion of the session's topic and readings*
○ *A role-play*
○ *Reflection on that session's reading. (The readings are found at the end of each of the ten sessions.)*
○ *Shared entries from the participants' "nonviolence journals."*
   The nonviolence journal is a good way for people to reflect on the issues, memories and questions that emerge for them during the course of the program. The nonviolence journal is confidential, but people are encouraged to voluntarily share one or more entries with the group if they feel comfortable doing so.

Notes to the Facilitator

○ In this guide, the facilitator is provided with a suggested curriculum for each two hour session. Each session is introduced by an agenda which outlines the topics that are dealt with during that gathering. This agenda indicates suggested times for each item, although often a topic may spark a great deal of discussion; we invite you to consider adjusting the agenda if this happens. Generally we have often provided more material than can often be dealt with in two hours. This allows you to choose from a range of possibilities in finalizing the agenda. Also, at the end of most of the sections you are provided with additional material; you may want to use some of this in place of the standard agenda, or use it in future sessions if the group wants to continue this process after Session Ten is completed.

❍ Each session includes suggested comments, prayers, presentations and instructions for the participants. Feel free to use them as printed or to put them into your own words.

❍ Please review the material for each session beforehand.

❍ Ask people to prepare for each session by reading all of its material: its lesson plan, supplemental material, and article(s). (All the materials for each session are found together.) Generally, this represents between ten and fifteen pages.

❍ For many sessions, you will need large pieces of paper taped on the wall and felt markers to record ideas coming from the group discussions.

❍ This book is designed so that facilitation may be shared. If it is appropriate, encourage the participants to facilitate one or more sessions.

❍ We encourage you to use music during these sessions.

❍ Participants are encouraged to watch videos on nonviolence between sessions.

❍ The *From Violence to Wholeness* team is available to answer any questions with regard to facilitating this program. Please feel free to contact us!

Acknowledgments

In 1993, Ken Butigan created a pilot project for the *From Violence To Wholeness* program, writing the original curriculum. In 1994, Patricia Bruno, O.P. joined the project. Their collaboration included the mutual development of the shape and content of parts of the present volume. Out of this creative, interactive process, Ken wrote this book while Patricia contributed to its editing and revision; she also assembled four of the readings that accompany the sections of these texts. In addition, she played a major role in the creation and promotion of this book by her enormous work on the project as its co-director for three years.

This curriculum draws directly on the thought and work of the entire Pace e Bene Franciscan Nonviolence Center community, including Alain Richard, OFM, Rosemary Lynch, OSF, Louis Vitale, OFM, Michele Fischer, SC, Mary Litell, OSF, Peter Ediger, Julia Occhiogrosso and Mary Morton. Much of the structure and content of this program has emerged from a series of week-long retreats Pace e Bene has hosted since 1992.

A special thanks to Cynthia Okayama Dopke and Christine Wilcox for copy-editing this manuscript.

Finally, we wish to acknowledge the many known and unknown women and men who have engaged in countless acts of active nonviolence. It is their examples of faith, love and passionate commitment which ground our ongoing experiment in this way of becoming more deeply human.

Additional Recommended Reading

In addition to the assigned readings for each session, the following texts provide a valuable introduction to active nonviolence.

John Dear, *The God of Peace: Toward a Theology of Nonviolence* (Maryknoll, NY: Orbis Books, 1994).

Richard Deats, "The Global Spread of Nonviolence," *Fellowship* (July/Augist 1996). Concise overview! Reprints available from FOR, Box 271, Nyack, NY 10960. 1 copy/$1.00.

James W. Douglass, *The Nonviolent Coming of God* (Maryknoll, NY: Orbis Books, 1991).

Pam McAllister, *You Can't Kill the Spirit: Stories of Women and Nonviolent Action* (Philadelphia: New Society Publishers, 1988).

Philip McManus and Gerald Schlabach, eds., *Relentless Persistence: Nonviolent Action in Latin America* (Philadelphia: New Society Publishers, 1991).

Bill Moyer, *The Practical Strategist.* (This is a superb resource -- it is available for $2.00 from the Social Movement Empowerment Project, 723 Shrader St., San Francisco, CA 94117.)

Angie O'Gorman, ed., *The Universe Bends Toward Justice: A Reader on Christian Nonviolence* (Philadelphia: New Society Publishers, 1991).

Roger S. Powers and William B. Vogele, eds., *Protest, Power, and Change: An Encyclopedia of Nonviolent Action from ACT-UP to Women's Suffrage* (New York, London: Garland Publishing Co, 1997).

Alain Richard, *Concerning Nonviolence and the Franciscan Movement* (Occasional Paper Series, No. 1, Las Vegas: NV: Pace e Bene, 1992 [1987]).

Elizabeth Schussler Fiorenza and Shawn Copeland, editors, *Violence Against Women* (Maryknoll, NY: Orbis Books, 1994).

Walter Wink, *Engaging the Powers: Discernment and Resistance in a World of Domination* (Minneapolis: Fortress, 1992). This is an especially important book! We strongly encourage participants to read this book during the *From Violence To Wholeness* Program.

Session 1

Beginning Our Journey From Violence To Wholeness

Session 1
Beginning Our Journey from Violence To Wholeness

Agenda

○ A prayer as we begin our journey [2 min.]

○ Introductions [15 min.]
○ Milling exercise [5 min.]
○ Small groups [20 min.]
○ Large group [15 min.]

○ The goals and process of the *From Violence To Wholeness* program [3 min.]
○ Starting points [10 min.]

○ Violence and nonviolence: an initial exploration [20 min.]
○ Describing active nonviolence [20 min.]

○ Conclusion [10 min.]

Supplemental Materials

A. Seven Starting Points
B. Supplementary Exercise on the Qualities of Nonviolence
C. Session 1 Reading:
   "The Decalogue for a Spirituality of Nonviolence,"
   by Rosemary Lynch, OSF and Alain Richard, OFM

Session 1

Beginning Our Journey
From Violence To Wholeness

A Prayer As We Begin Our Journey -- 2 min.

Spirit of God,
we long to mend the broken circle.
We long to heal the fractures in the world around us
and within our own souls.
To learn from one another the ways of living fully alive.
To transform those parts of ourselves and our world
that block our making contact with our deepest reality and with the
deepest, richest and most sacred dimensions of all other beings.

Spirit of God, we long to see reality.
To contact our deepest yearning for a world pulsing with justice and truth.
To dream of a society where we all sit down at the Great Banquet,
where every person eats until they are full.

Spirit of God, we long to discover anew the courage deep within us.
To see and to listen. To discover our true selves.
To take steps to stop the cycle of violence
in our homes, in our work-places, in our neighborhoods, in our country,
and in our entire world.

Introductions — 15 min.

Tape several pieces of paper on the wall. Invite each person one at a time to come forward and use a felt-tip pen to write out their full name. Ask them to explain briefly where each name came from and what they prefer to be called. Ask people to take a minute or so. To get the ball rolling, it's a good idea for the facilitator to model this.

The advantage of this process of introductions is that people get a chance to share something personal, but not too personal. It creates a sense of commonality and usually good feeling — often people relate humorous facts about their names. And it is a simple but powerful way to bring into the room our families and heritages.

After the last person has shared, comment on how this sharing has called to mind our families, our roots, and all who have gone before us. Explain how, by sharing in this way, we have recalled their experiments in resolving the dilemmas of life in human and nonviolent ways, and we imagine how they long for us to help create a more human and nonviolent world now.

If the group is larger than 10 people, do this reflection in two groups.

Milling Exercise — 5 min.

Milling is a way to form small groups of four persons each. Ask people to stand up and begin milling about, as if they are on a busy and crowded street corner. After 30 seconds, have them stop. Ask each person to join with one other person in silence. Ask them to be present together, but not in an uncomfortable way (e.g., they should not feel forced to look into each other's eyes). Read the first statement in the milling section below; have people begin the process again, and then read the second statement. Ask the current couple to join another one, thus forming a group of four.

After the first milling, say:

❍ The person standing before you has likely experienced the harshness of life, with its difficulties, its times of unfairness, and its moments of sorrow and loss. This person has likely experienced some forms of violence — perhaps emotional violence, perhaps verbal violence, perhaps physical violence. Be quietly aware of the life journey of the person standing before you, especially her or his likely experiences of violence. *(A moment of silence)* ...Now, acknowledge this person in some way, and then let us start our milling again.

After the second milling, say:

❍ The person standing before you has been on a spiritual journey all through her or his entire life. Faced with adversity, with loss, with her or his own woundedness, they have been on a journey toward wholeness and meaning. They have been on a journey toward the fullness of love. They have been experimenting with love, even in the most difficult of times. Let us quietly be aware of the length and breadth and depth of their journey toward becoming human. *(A moment of silence)* ...Now, let us acknowledge this person in some way.

Now, I invite each couple to join with another couple in order to form a four-person group.

Small Groups — 20 min.

Ask the small groups to reflect on the following questions. Invite them to share <u>at whatever level they feel comfortable</u>.

❍ Why do you want to learn more about nonviolence?

○ When you think back over your life, do you recall an experience which had anything to do with this question of violence or nonviolence?

Large Group Discussion — 15 min.

Ask people to reassemble in the large group and share an experience or insight that emerged during the small group reflection.

The Goals and Process of *From Violence To Wholeness* -- 3 min.

Take this time to introduce the From Violence To Wholeness program:

From Violence To Wholeness is a step-by-step process which helps us deepen our knowledge of nonviolence and to assemble a kit of nonviolent tools which we can use every day to put that knowledge into practice.

Through this program, we explore ways to address the conflicts in our lives and the life of the world. Our goal is to become familiar with ways to resolve these conflicts by using creative, persistent, and grounded nonviolence.

This program consists of ten sessions. In each session, we will cultivate our grounding in nonviolence through prayer, reflection on scripture, small group discussions, role play, selected reading, and presentations. We ask that you attend all the sessions and do the basic reading. We also encourage you to keep a nonviolence journal during the program.

Drawing on Christianity's peace and justice tradition, Christian feminism and Gandhi's nonviolence of "soul-force," this program explores ways through which we can give expression to our true selves in every part of our lives.

This program honors your life experience. It assumes that, one way or another, you have been making choices for nonviolence throughout your life. You may not have called it "nonviolence," but there have been experiences in your life when you have addressed conflict with creativity or when you have taken initiative to break the cycle of violence. This program recognizes that we stand at the midpoint of this nonviolent journey rather than at the beginning.

Finally, you are invited to participate in this program at whatever level you feel comfortable. Nonviolence often calls us to reflect on our experience. We seek to create a safe space in which to do this. In that spirit, we ask you to share only what you freely wish to share. The facilitator, in general, is not a trained psychotherapist or a counselor. We are not here to psychoanalyze one another. *This is not therapy.* We are people of faith working together to become more deeply grounded in nonviolence. If something comes up for you that goes beyond the scope of this program, we invite you to address this with a professional therapist.

Starting Points — 10 min.

*Share and invite discussion of the following two "starting points."
These two points are part of a larger list found in this section's "Supple-
mental Material." Invite people to read the entire list of
"Starting Points" (pp. 16-17) between now and the next session.*

1. We don't have to be perfectly nonviolent before we can take action! Nonviolence is something we *grow into*.

Fr. Alain Richard — Pace e Bene staff member and a Franciscan
priest who has been engaged in nonviolent activities for much of his life
— says, "Just because I talk about nonviolence doesn't mean that I *am*
nonviolent. I will probably not be *really* nonviolent until fifteen minutes
after I am dead!" What he is indicating is that nonviolence is something
we construct and grow into. It is not a state of idealistic perfection. As
Gandhi stressed, nonviolence is a continual series of "experiments with
truth" through which we gradually learn how to become more human.

2. Active nonviolence is a spiritual journey.

Addressing the violence in our lives and the life of the world
launches us on a journey which brings us face to face with our illusions
as well as the source of love and compassion which transforms and heals
all wounds. It is a journey from despair to hope, from fear to grace,
from fragmentation to our truest selves. It is therefore not something
purely mechanical, where one simply applies a particular technique.
Tools are useful — and we will explore them in this program — but
ultimately they must be rooted in the ground of being, the merciful and
replenishing love of the Nonviolent God who longs for our wholeness as
individuals and as a community.

Violence and Nonviolence: An Initial Exploration — 10 min.

*Ask a participant to read the following passage from John 14: 27 (New
American Bible) as a way of centering our exploration of violence and
nonviolence:*

"Peace I leave with you;
my peace I give to you.
Not as the world gives do I give it to you.
Do not let your heart be troubled or afraid."

John 14:27 (New American Bible)

*Begin this exploration with a large group discussion of the elements of
violence. First read aloud:*

Active nonviolence does not pretend that we live in a world that is free of violence. Instead, it seeks to confront and transform the violence in our lives and all around us. Thus, it is important to understand what violence is and how it works. Let's brainstorm on what characterizes violence.

Record ideas on large sheet of paper or blackboard. After the group has come up with several dimensions of violence, ask a participant to read the following descriptions of violence:

○ *Violence* is emotional, verbal, or physical behavior which dominates, diminishes, or destroys ourselves or others.
○ *Violence* crosses boundaries without permission, disrupts authentic relationships, and separates us from other beings.
○ *Violence* is often motivated by fear, unrestrained anger, or greed to increase domination or power over others. It can also be motivated by a desire for justice in the face of injustice: a longing to put things right, to overcome an imbalance of power, to end victimization or oppression. Often, those who perpetrate violence do so with the conviction that they are overcoming a prior violence or injustice. In this program, we will explore whether or not there are alternative ways to achieve true justice.
○ *Violence* often provokes new violence. This spiral of retaliatory violence is often propelled by social or personal scripts that are enacted in situations of conflict.

Describing Active Nonviolence -- 20 min.

Introduce this section with the beginning paragraph and ask participants to read the following descriptions of active nonviolence:

Active nonviolence is a process which seeks to resolve conflict in a humane and effective way. Thus, as we begin our program together, let us consider some of the elements of this definition of active nonviolence, into which we will delve more deeply in the coming sessions:

○ Active nonviolence is a creative, powerful, and effective process for addressing and resolving conflict.
○ Active nonviolence seeks to break the spiral of violence and to create options for a more human alternative.
○ Active nonviolence is an act of faith in the Nonviolent God; it is a powerful means of experiencing this God.
○ Active nonviolence holds that human beings are meant to love and be loved.
○ For active nonviolence, reality is one. The nonviolence practitioner therefore yearns to transform all that separates human beings from themselves, from one another and from the earth.
○ Active nonviolence seeks the truth: the opponent's truth as well as one's own.

13

○ Active nonviolence acknowledges the woundedness, the violence, and the sacredness of ourselves and others.

○ Active nonviolence is a process of repentance and transformation.

○ Active nonviolence is a spiritual journey from fear, despair and greed to compassion, balance and wholeness.

Invite the group to reflect on these descriptions of active nonviolence.

Then reflect on the "The Decalogue for a Spirituality of Nonviolence," by Rosemary Lynch, O.S.F. and Alain Richard, O.F.M., located at the end of this section.

Conclusion — 10 min.

Nonviolence Journal

○ *Encourage participants to keep a nonviolence journal during this program. Ask them to write on any topic related to violence and non-violence, especially their own experiences, issues, struggles.*

> *Although these journals are confidential, encourage them to occasionally share an entry if they feel comfortable doing so. As you will notice in the agenda for each session, there is a time for sharing at the beginning.*

> *We have provided topics in each session on which the participants can work.*

Offer this nonviolence journal topic for the next session:

Please reflect on two experiences:
1. One where you inflicted violence, and
2. One where it was inflicted on you.

Readings

○ *Ask participants to read all the material for the next session:*
   1) The lesson plan for Session 2
   2) The supplemental material of both Session 1 and Session 2, and
   3) Session 2's reading: John Dear, "Forgetting Who We Are"

Evaluation

○ *Hold a brief evaluation of this session:*
1. *First, ask people to share the things that worked well, and*
2. *Ask them to share things that could be improved.*

Closing Circle

Ask people to stand and form a circle. In the spirit of prayer, close with the following:

In this program, we will explore the vision and techniques of nonviolence. These are important, but by themselves they are useless. Ultimately, they must be animated and guided by the power of God's reconciling love. The spirit of the unifying God is present when conflict is resolved; when the script of violence is re-written to allow us to embrace the sacredness of those against whom we struggle; when creativity is used to break the spiral of retaliation.

The techniques discussed in this program flourish when they are rooted in the spirituality that Jesus taught and lived. This spirituality proclaims that all beings are in the embrace of the Nonviolent God, the One who longs for our wholeness and unity. This spirituality testifies that God is our foundation, our source, the Ground of our being and all Being. This spirituality maintains that nothing is impossible for God, including the healing of the deepest violence and injury. This spirituality announces that our vocation as Christians is to be instruments of peace and justice in every moment of our lives. It asserts that the church is the place where ordinary women and men ought to gather to learn, and receive support for carrying this ministry of nonviolence out into our lives and the life of the world.

In the following sessions, we will explore together how to bring this spirituality of active nonviolence, love and justice alive. Amen.

Session 1: Supplemental Material

A. Seven Starting Points

1. We don't have to be perfectly nonviolent! Nonviolence is something we *grow into*.

Fr. Alain Richard — Pace e Bene staff member and a Franciscan priest who has been engaged in nonviolent activities for much of his life — says, "Just because I talk about nonviolence doesn't mean that I *am* nonviolent. I will probably not be *really* nonviolent until fifteen minutes after I am dead!" What he is indicating is that nonviolence is something we construct and grow into. It is not a state of idealistic perfection. As Gandhi stressed, nonviolence is a continual series of "experiments with truth" through which we gradually learn how to be human.

2. Nonviolence does not assume that the world is nonviolent.

Sometimes we think that for nonviolence to be effective, the whole world has to somehow become nonviolent. Active nonviolence does not hold to this illusion. In fact, it assumes that the world is often violent and unjust. Real nonviolence does not attempt to create a world where there is no conflict. *It recognizes that we face conflict all through our lives.* This program explores the ways in which nonviolence is a more effective means of addressing and resolving conflict than violence.

3. Active nonviolence takes the reality of evil very seriously. But it takes the reality of good even more seriously.

Nonviolence does not pretend that evil does not exist. Nevertheless, it does not subscribe to the belief that evil is the bottom line, that it is the ultimate reality. Active nonviolence maintains that the picture we receive every day from the media is *not* the entire truth. Active nonviolence challenges this incomplete and false picture of life and maintains that, while violence is a fact, the world also rings with love, courage and grace which are ultimately greater than violence and are capable of transforming it.

4. Nonviolence begins with taking responsibility for our own state of mind, feelings, and actions.

In most conflicts, we have two different ways of responding. The first is to react defensively. Often we do this by instantaneously acting out deeply ingrained "conflict scripts." The second way is to allow our true self to take action. This is the way of active nonviolence.

Nonviolence is not primarily a way to armor ourselves against others. This can produce feelings of victimization and this, in turn, can justify our using violence in return. Instead, it is a means of creating a situation that stops the immediate violence, clarifies the real issues, and produces a resolution. Ultimately, this means taking responsibility for our own behavior, no matter what others do.

5. Active nonviolence can be used to respond to every level of violence.

We are challenged to experiment with active nonviolence in the face of many manifestations of violence. These include interpersonal violence, violence in the work place, violence between differing communities, violence against the Earth. These also include the overarching structures of violence that consciously and unconsciously shape and inform our personal and social lives in profoundly disturbing ways, including economic violence, racism, and sexism. The nonviolence practitioner seeks creative and relentlessly persistent ways to use nonviolent methods to transform these conditions and their underlying assumptions and attitudes.

6. We need support to put active nonviolence into practice.

Nonviolence is a process of seeing and challenging patterns of violence and injustice. To do this well, we need each other. We need communities of people who are seeking to transform their own violence and the violence around them. We need safe space to reflect on this process with others. We need allies with whom we can practice these methods, and people with whom we can debrief. We need companions when we take nonviolent action. In general, nonviolence is not a solitary activity.

7. Active nonviolence is a spiritual journey.

Addressing the violence in our lives and in the life of the world in a deeply human and nonviolent way means undertaking a journey which brings us face to face with our illusions as well as the source of love and compassion that transforms and heals all wounds. It is a journey from despair to hope, from fear to grace, from fragmentation to our true selves. It is therefore not something purely mechanical, where one simply applies a particular technique. Tools are useful — and we will explore them in this program — but ultimately they must be rooted in the ground of being, the merciful and replenishing love of the Nonviolent God who longs for our wholeness as individuals and as a community.

B. Exercise on the Qualities of Nonviolence

Ask the large group to share various stereotypes which people in our society have about nonviolence and the people who practice it. (For example: "passive," "door-mat," "ineffective," "utopian," "unpatriotic," "unrealistic," "unemployed.") Write them on a large piece of paper on the wall. Reflect with the group about this list. Point out that it is important to identify these judgments for two reasons:

1. A certain kind of nonviolence has sometimes contributed to these attitudes. It is therefore important to distinguish between stereotypes about nonviolence and the active nonviolence we want to explore in this program; and

2. Most of us, at some level of awareness, share some or all of these interpretations. It is important therefore to raise them and address them, rather than pretending that these objections do not exist. Often, it is these attitudes which subvert and destroy a genuine nonviolence.

Next, ask people to articulate a list of qualities or attributes of people who practice nonviolence. (Often, such a list includes qualities like "courageous," "creative," "centered," "determined," "passionate," "disarming.") Underline the contrast between the two lists. Reflect on what the second list suggests about the depth and richness of active nonviolence.

The Decalogue for a Spirituality of Nonviolence

By Rosemary Lynch, OSF and Alain Richard, OFM

Active nonviolence calls us:

1. To learn to recognize and respect *"the sacred"* ("that of God" as the Quakers say) in every person, including in ourselves, and in every piece of Creation. The acts of the nonviolent person help to free this *Divine* in the opponent from obscurity or captivity.

2. To accept oneself deeply, "who I am" with all my gifts and richness, with all my limitations, errors, failings and weaknesses, and to realize that I am accepted by God. To live in the truth of ourselves, without excessive pride, with fewer delusions and false expectations.

3. To recognize that what I resent, and perhaps even detest, in another, comes from my difficulty in admitting that this same reality lives also in me. To recognize and renounce my own violence, which becomes evident when I begin to monitor my words, gestures, reactions.

4. To renounce dualism, the "we-they" mentality (Manicheism). This divides us into "good people/bad people" and allows us to demonize the adversary. It is the root of authoritarian and exclusivist behavior. It generates racism and makes possible conflicts and wars.

5. To face fear and to deal with it not mainly with courage but with love.

6. To understand and accept that the *New Creation*, the building up of the *Beloved Community* is always carried forward with others. It is never a "solo act." This requires patience and the ability to pardon.

7. To see ourselves as a part of the whole creation to which we foster a relationship of love, not of mastery, remembering that the destruction of our planet is a profoundly spiritual problem, not simply a scientific or technological one. *We are one.*

8. To be ready to suffer, perhaps even with joy, if we believe this will help liberate the *Divine* in others. This includes the acceptance of our place and moment in history with its trauma, with its ambiguities.

9. To be capable of celebration, of joy, when the presence of God has been accepted, and when it has not been to help discover and recognize this fact.

10. To slow down, to be patient, planting the seeds of love and forgiveness in our own hearts and in the hearts of those around us. Slowly we will grow in love, compassion and the capacity to forgive.

Session 2

The Experience and Dynamics of Violence

Session 2
The Experience and Dynamics of Violence

Agenda

○ Opening prayer [2 min.]

○ Reflections since the last session [8 min.]
○ Small groups [20 min.]
○ Large group [15 min.]

○ A violence/nonviolence barometer [15 min.]
○ Large group [10 min.]

○ Reflecting on the reading, "Forgetting Who We Are"
   by John Dear [10 min.]

○ Group brainstorm: What kinds of violence are there? [10 min.]
○ Two basic ways of responding to violence [10 min.]
○ Large group discussion: The violence system in action [15 min.]

○ Conclusion [5 min.]

Supplemental Materials

A. Some Principles of Violence
B. Milling Exercise
C. Existential roots of violence: The fear of death
D. Additional recommended readings
E. Session 2 Reading: "Forgetting Who We Are," by John Dear, S.J

Session 2
The Experience and Dynamics of Violence

Opening Prayer — 2 min.

We huddle together
as the storm shrieks around us and through us.
The storm of misguided power,
of icy blindness and abuse,
of the deep gulf that widens between us,
of the suffocating pathos, of the paralyzing unease we feel
when we are rejected and disposed of,
or when we reject and dispose of others.
Tossed by the storm where we lose our
particularity and our irreducible richness.
Savaged by the storm that is inflicted on us, and that we inflict.
We ask for the means to live fully in the midst of this storm,
to embark on this challenging and difficult and powerful journey
from fear to love, from despair to hope,
from violence to wholeness.

Reflections Since the Last Session — 8 min.

Take a few minutes to reflect together on issues or experiences which this program has raised for the participants since the last gathering. Ask people if they would like to volunteer to share an excerpt from their nonviolence journals.

Small Groups — 20 min.

Members of the small groups are invited to reflect on the following — again, at whatever level each person feels comfortable:

○ Please reflect on one experience where you inflicted violence or where it was inflicted on you.

Large Group — 15 min.

Ask people to reassemble in the large group and to share an experience or insight that emerged during the small group reflection.

A Violence/Nonviolence Barometer — 15 min.

This game -- developed by Peace Brigades International and other groups -- often reveals the range of opinions a group holds about violence and nonviolence. It often raises a range of important questions about what violence is and how it works.

Have the group get up and move the chairs and tables to the sides of the room. Mark an imaginary line down the middle of the room with chairs or other objects. One side of the line is designated "violent," while the other side is "not violent." The farther away from the line, the more "violent" or "not violent" it is. Closer to the line, the situation is more ambiguous. If a person is not sure, they can straddle the line.

Read one of the scenarios below and ask if the action of the person in the scenario is violent or nonviolent. Ask people to occupy a place in relationship to the dividing line, depending on their position. The facilitator then asks people why they are standing where they are. One of the rules is that the participants can adjust their location if what someone else says helps them change their minds. Everyone's opinion should be respected.

Here are some scenarios, some of which have been developed by Quakers in the United States. Use at least two of them, or create your own:

1) Alice has greatly insulted Jon. In turn, Jon has shut Alice out of his life and refuses to acknowledge her existence. Is Jon's action violent or not violent?

2) Gloria spray paints "this insults women" on a sexist billboard. Is her action violent or not violent?

3) A person does nothing as a man on a nearby street repeatedly slaps a woman who appears to be his wife or girlfriend. Is the bystander's action violent or not violent?

4) A company with a sizable profit margin decides to relocate to Mexico in order to increase its profits even further. This will cost a small town 200 jobs. Is this company's actions violent or not violent?

5) A large corporation has many product lines. One of them is weapons, including land mines. Your church calls for an international boycott of the company's products. Is the church's action violent or not violent?

6) Sylvia and Rick, led by their conscience, clandestinely enter a nuclear missile factory and use household hammers to disable a nuclear warhead. Is their action violent or not violent?

7) Greg spanks a child who is misbehaving. Is his action violent or not violent?

8) A Roman Catholic U.S. Air Force pilot during a recent war bombed an

air-raid shelter, killing 400 civilians. His bishop has a private meeting with him, asking him to repent this sin of murder. He tells him that, otherwise, he will be excommunicated from the church.

The pilot explains that he had not sinned; that it was war-time and that he was following a legitimate order; and that therefore he would not repent his actions. The following day, the bishop announced during a press conference that the pilot has been excommunicated from the church. Is the bishop's action violent or nonviolent?

Large Group — 20 min.

Ask the group to reassemble to reflect on this exercise. Then ask: What is the range of violent phenomena? Reflect on how violence can be emotional, verbal, and physical; how it is personal, interpersonal, and structural. Examples:

O Domestic violence.

O Violence in the workplace.

O Racism.

O Sexism.

O Structural economic violence.

O Violence against the earth.

O International armed conflict.

Then, ask the group to read, one by one, the descriptions of violence we first looked at in Session One:

O *Violence* is emotional, verbal, or physical behavior which dominates, diminishes, dehumanizes or destroys ourselves or others.
O *Violence* crosses boundaries without permission, disrupts authentic relationships, and separates us from other beings.
O *Violence* is often motivated by fear, unrestrained anger, or greed to increase domination or power over others. It can also be motivated by a desire for justice in the face of injustice: a longing to put things right, to overcome an imbalance of power, to end victimization or oppression. Often, those who perpetrate violence do so with the conviction that they are overcoming a prior violence or injustice.
O *Violence* often provokes new violence. This spiral of retaliatory violence is often propelled by social or personal scripts that are enacted in situations of conflict.

Reflecting on this Session's Reading:
"Forgetting Who We Are" (John Dear) — 10 min.

Ask the group to articulate and discuss some of the key insights of the article. Here are some of the key points.

○ "Violence is best defined as that act of forgetting or ignoring who we are: brothers and sisters of one another, each one of us a child of God."

○ "Violence is any behavior that dehumanizes us, from thoughts of self-hatred to intentional harm or physical injury done to another."

○ "Our apathy and indifference in the face of relievable suffering and our willingness to defend our possessions and self-interests have harmful effects on others and are a participation in violence."

○ "Once we forget who we are and begin to act violently, we start to legitimize what we do and to systematize our wickedness."
Ask the group: What are some of the ways we do this?

○ "In the spiral of violence, the perception of another as 'enemy' stimulates the use of violence.... Charles McCarthy defines an enemy as 'one or many who negatively affect the survival of some self-interest,' such as life, possessions, reputation or power."
Ask people to reflect on this definition of "the enemy."

Then ask the group:
How does this idea of "the enemy" contribute to the spiral of violence?
What examples can you think of?

Two Basic Ways of Responding to Violence -- 10 min.

Present these ideas:

There are two general categories of responding to violence:

A) To accommodate violence, to avoid it, or to use violence to fight violence, or:

B) The tradition of cooperation and active nonviolence.

Let's look at the first category:

1) Accommodating violence is a common and traditional way of responding to violence.

This approach sees no other option but passivity or silence. It goes along with violence. It maintains that there is nothing that can be done about this violence. This point of view holds that violence is the bottom line. It is the way things are. Passivity and silence often seem the most sensible approach.

Ask the group: Does this resonate with your experience? Have you found yourself doing this? Is this your usual response? Can you think of a situation like this?

Then, resume reflecting on this topic:

The problem with accommodating violence is that it is demeaning and dehumanizing. It reinforces a relationship that is fatally out of balance. It keeps an inhuman situation intact, where one person is above another. We become defined and dealt with in terms of our roles: the dominator and the dominated. This is demeaning and dehumanizing to the one who is dominated, but it is also demeaning and dehumanizing to the dominator. Why? Because for both of them, this imbalance creates more and more distance from their true selves. It gets them stuck in a role, in a movie script, that keeps them from making contact with their true selves and the true selves of others. Because of this, the dominator/dominated model makes it more difficult to ultimately change this situation — that is, to bring this relationship into balance.

2) Another traditional method of dealing with violence is avoidance.

Avoidance means standing on the sidelines, to evade "getting involved," to decide it's not "my problem," or to deputize someone else (the police, the army) to deal with it. It is the act of becoming a bystander. This is what we mean by *avoiding* it — avoiding having to deal with the root conflict or to deal with the consequences, especially if others are bearing those consequences. Instead, we flee from the conflict.

Ask the group: Does this resonate with your experience? Have you found yourself doing this? Is this your usual response? Can you think of a situation like this?

Then, resume reflecting on this:

The difficulty with this approach is that it does not resolve the problem at hand, and it creates the illusion that we can stay "above the fray" and not face the conflicts in our lives and in the life of the world.

3) The third traditional response to violence is to use counter-violence.

This approach maintains that there is no other option, and that violence only ends through a show of greater violent force.

Ask the group: Let's take a minute and silently ask ourselves: Does this resonate with your experience? Have you found yourself doing this? Is this your usual response? Can you think of a situation like this?

Then, resume reflecting on this:

The problems with this method are that it reinforces the cycle of retaliatory violence; it does not address the roots of conflict; and it does not create a solution that meets the needs of the parties involved. Not only does it prolong suffering, it is often ineffective.

Use these thoughts to conclude this discussion:

A key to nonviolence is noticing our habits of thought — becoming aware of our typical way or style of addressing conflict or violence. By doing this, we can see the script we use, and then can begin to re-write this script.

Is there an alternative to these typical ways of responding? Yes — the tradition of cooperation and active nonviolence.

Large Group Discussion: The Violence System in Action -- 15 min.

Have the large group reflect on all the different factors that contribute to the violence in the following scenario:

A man has just been laid off from his job, the victim of corporate downsizing. He had worked for the company for 15 years. In the past two years there had been a series of layoffs. Once at home, he gets into an argument with his wife. During their argument he hits her.

Ask people to identify all the social or personal patterns that might be involved in this violence. Some of the factors might include:

○ The male identity or role that he has been educated into all his life, including attitudes toward people and himself.
Ask people what that might include: attitudes about women, attitudes about male authority, the role of violence in personal relationships, etc.

○ The individual pattern of relating the husband and wife have constructed and reinforced during their time together

○ The attitude of the corporation to its workers

○ The economic structures of society

○ The cultural assumptions that maintain and reinforce these economic structures (e.g., consumerism, competition, superiority)

Conclusion — 5 min.

Nonviolence Journal

○ *Offer this nonviolence journal topic for the next session:*

Please reflect on any experience where you felt the persons involved were using nonviolence to resolve a conflict.

Readings

○ *Remind participants to read all the material for the next session:*
1) The lesson plan for Session 3
2) The supplemental material for Session 3, and
3) "The Faithful Nonviolence of Jesus," by Nancy Schreck.

Evaluation

○ *Hold a brief evaluation of this session:*
1. First, ask people to share the things that worked well, and
2. Ask them to share things that could be improved.

Closing Circle

○ *Closing circle: offer a brief reflection or prayer on facing the dynamics of violence in our own lives.*

A. <u>Some Principles of Violence</u>

1) Violent acts are part of a larger "violence system."

Violence is often carried out by individuals, but violence cannot be understood only as individual behavior. As individuals we commit violence and we share responsibility for this violence. But we are also living in the midst of what biblical scholar Walter Wink calls a "domination system," a set of values, assumptions, structures and cultural conditions that actively corrode and retard our humanity. This domination system depends on what Wink calls the "myth of redemptive violence."

Wink's scholarly research shows that the "domination system" is a likely translation of what Jesus calls "cosmos" or "world" in the New Testament. When Jesus says, "I am *in* the world but not *of* the world," Wink holds that a more apt translation rends this line, "I am *in* the domination system but not *of* the domination system." Jesus lives in the midst of this system of domination, but does not belong to it. This system is found in structures of organized fear, destructive power, greed, hatred, and despair, but also in their underlying values which we experience both within us and outside us, both in our personal lives and in the life of the world.

Like every world-view, the domination system claims to be ultimate Reality. This belief-system maintains that violence is the ultimate logic and law of the universe. In this world-view violence is "the way things are," "the bottom line," the "real world." This world-view implies that even the God of love is subject to its logic. If we consciously or unconsciously accept this world-view as Reality, our identity and behavior flow from it. *Every violent action is an act of faith in the domination system.*

In this program, we will call this system the "violence system."

2) The violence system maintains that human beings are essentially violent, and that violence is irreversible.

According to this belief system, human beings are violators: we are meant to violate and be violated by others. Therefore, human beings have *no choice* but to conduct their lives violently. Life is thus one long spiral of violence, victimization, and counter-violence. According to this belief, there is no escape from this cycle. Life is a closed system. Violence is irreversible: only passivity or retaliation are available to us, thus ruling out true conflict resolution, forgiveness, and reconciliation. For the domination system, only violence can answer violence.

3) The violence system manifests itself in a series of interlocking war zones.

Where this logic prevails, it creates zones of domination and violence: within one's own being, interpersonally, between groups, structurally, between nations, and against the earth. These war zones reinforce one another and thus reinforce the general domination system. They seek to convince us that this is all there is.

4) The violence system heralds violence as the solution to conflict and as a means of human fulfillment.

The domination system uses violence as its fundamental tactic to defend or strengthen the individual and societal ego. Propelled by fear — ultimately the fear of death — the domination system maintains that human beings can only survive and thrive by overtly or covertly dominating, manipulating, or threatening others.

5) The violence system objectifies and separates human beings.

Domination requires objectifying and separating others. In US society, for example, this is represented in a series of general assumptions of "superiority." For example, the dominant culture assumes that men are superior to women; white people are superior to people of color; wealthy people are superior to poor people; the US is superior to other nations, especially those of the so-called Third World; and human beings are superior to nature.

6) The violence system legitimates new acts of dominance and violence.

The violence system justifies, and is justified by, the perpetual re-enactment of the violence cycle. Nonviolence is said to be discredited when it does not always "work." Violence never seems to have this problem. No matter how many times violence fails to resolve conflict, it is rarely discredited.

7) The spiral of violence is propelled by the "violence scripts" used by individuals and by society.

Generally, we confront conflict by drawing on patterns, myths and presuppositions we have been taught (through word and deed) by our families and our cultures. The "violence script" is a very old and predictable script. The script of retaliatory and escalating violence creates a well-grooved neural pathway within ourselves and our society.

When we face situations that provoke fear, anxiety, anger or greed, these pathways are stimulated in a way we think is "spontaneous" and "natural." Often, we have been ratifying these patterns all our lives. When we face a crisis, we feel that we have no choice but to travel down that path. This script deludes us into thinking this is natural, when in fact it is a construct we maintain and deepen. This leads us to believe that violence is the only choice we have when faced with conflict or violence.

C. Existential Roots of Violence: The Fear of Death — 5 min.

Our cultures teach us the "script" of violence as a way of waging a conflict. Ernest Becker, in his book *The Denial of Death* (Boston: The Free Press, 1973), maintains that what ultimately drives our use of violence is our fear of death. By definition, we as mortal beings are going to die, and this reality pervades our life. It is such a contradiction that we can be so creatively alive, and yet we are destined to lose our lives. The fear of death, the fear of losing our very self, grounds all our other fears.

Becker says that, in response, we devise many ways to deny this most basic reality. One of the most pervasive ways of creating the illusion of invulnerability is to inflict death on others. We believe, writes Becker, that we can somehow forestall our own death by killing others. We come to believe that meting out extinction makes us supremely powerful because we ourselves are not extinguished. Every act of violence — emotional, verbal or physical — intimates or symbolizes this infliction of death on our opponents. Is this the basis of patriarchy?

Following this line of thinking, confronting our violence ultimately means confronting our fears, including this most wrenching fear of our own mortality.

D. Additional Recommended Readings

Elizabeth Schussler Fiorenza and Shawn Copeland, editors, *Women Against Violence* (Maryknoll, NY: Orbis Books, 1994).
Walter Wink, Chapters 1-5, and 7, *Engaging the Powers: Discernment and Resistance in a World of Domination* (Minneapolis: Fortress, 1992), pp 13-104 and 139-155.

Session 2 Reading:

Forgetting Who We Are

by John Dear, SJ

We lined up in a long row behind the old blue bus. I stood in the middle of the highway along with fifty or so Salvadoran *campesinos* [farmworkers]who were traveling in El Salvador to the town of Chalatenango. Our bus was stopped and searched by the army. All the women were forced to line up in front of the bus. It was a Sunday after- noon and there was not another sign of life as far as we could see. We were in the middle of barren fields, surrounded by huge mountains far away on the horizon. We were somewhere in the north of El Salvador and we were surrounded by young Salvadoran soldiers with machine guns aimed at us.

It was a normal road check. The soldiers were looking for guerril- las or weapons that were being transported. But there was fear in the air; the weapons were meant to intimidate and to protect. I realized that any kind of accident could happen and I looked to see how the other Salvador- ans alongside me were responding. They simply bowed their heads and stood in silence. We were all searched one by one and questioned as to our reasons for traveling in this part of the country. After a while, we were permitted to get back on the bus and we proceeded on our way.

On that day in El Salvador, I saw brothers and sisters acting toward one another as if they were objects or things to be feared or pushed around. I saw children of God sadly trapped into a way of life, dehumaniz- ing one another and themselves.

Violence is best defined as that act of forgetting or ignoring who we are: brothers and sisters of one another, each one of us a child of God. Violence occurs in those moments when we forget and deny our basic identity as God's children, when we treat one another as if we were worth- less instead of priceless and cling to our own selfish desires, possessions and security. It can become a trap, a way of life in which we see no way out, in which we find no hope, in which we become unable to look into one another's eyes with love and respect. Violence is any behavior that dehu- manizes us, from thoughts of self-hatred to intentional harm or physical injury done to another. Our apathy and indifference in the face of relievable suffering and our willingness to defend our possessions and self-interests have harmful effects on others and are a participation in violence. The lack of love and the anxiety in our hearts, the unwillingness to suffer with others and to forgive others, and the insecurity, the fears and untruth in which we frame our lives are all participations in violence because their consequences are harmful to others.

Violence begins in our hearts when we give in to temptation and become anxious and fearful, when we lose inner peace and harmony. As we forget or ignore the reality that we are all equal, all children of a loving God, all brothers and sisters of one another, our hearts turn from truth and love. This negative state of forgetfulness feeds on itself and soon we find ourselves lying, hating and cheating others. Our communication with others is disrupted and we act as if we do not recognize who the other person is or who other people are. Any common ground of equality or understanding vanishes. We become unable to see the world from the perspective of others and we cling to our own absolute idea of right and wrong. In our self-centeredness, we become blind and unconcerned about others, especially those who are suffering.

When we characterize another or others as enemies, when we look with fear and suspicion at others, we reveal the violence in our own hearts, the fact that we have forgotten to whom we are relating. When we respond to threats or acts of violence by using violence or by passively receiving the violence, we act in ways that go against what is good for us, what we would truly desire if we only understood the fact of our common heritage as sons and daughters of God. In the spiral of violence, the perception of another as "enemy" stimulates the use of violence which in turn encourages that other person or group to label the initiators of the violence as "enemy." Charles McCarthy defines an enemy as "one or many who negatively affect the survival of some self-interest," such as life, possessions, reputation or power.[1] An "enemy" poses a threat of harm to oneself, or to one's values, friends or possessions, or may have already committed violence toward oneself or one's self-interest. Quarrels and conflicts begin when opposing people insist and scream at each other: "I'm absolutely right." With this absolute conviction and unwillingness to listen, people feel justified in harming and then killing one another.

Once we forget who we are and begin to act violently, we start to legitimize what we do and to systematize our wickedness. We keep working at this legitimization to defend our perceptions, our use of violence. With the systemic violence of society, we try to encourage one another to accept violence. The way of violence becomes a habit too hard to break. Sometimes we find ourselves in situations where we defend our use of violence and we are unable to break the habit, unable to change, unable to risk another way of life. We adopt patriotic and nationalistic symbols and ideologies which can divide us and we get caught in an uncontrollable, unreflected spirit which separates us and divides us from the whole human family. Soon we lose any faith in God and do not believe in the reality of the human family. Once we find ourselves in such an apparently hopeless situation, we can fall into greater despair, helplessness and self-hatred.

We create idols which take the place of the one true God, since by this time we have lost any sight of God's presence in the other person. Idolatry is our denial of God's existence in others and the placing of our faith and trust in anything or anyone other than God. Our new idols become our only security, our way of defending the forgetfulness, the lie that we are living in and the violence that we do. The nuclear arms race, for example, is the practice of idolatry: people have placed their faith, trust and dependence on nuclear weapons and not in God. We have forgotten that we are one family, have greedily pursued selfish interests, and have produced nuclear weapons to protect our possessions. The end result of this denial of God has been the violence committed against the poor who starve and suffer disease, illiteracy, and homelessness. Wealth, the desire for honor, and pride kill the Spirit in each of us, cause systemic violence against the poor, and lead to new and bigger idolatries in our world, such as the nuclear arms race, consumerism, abortion, sexism and classism.

Charles McCarthy defines violence specifically as "responding to a person as an object for the purpose of self-gratification. Violence is forgetting or ignoring that there is an infinity behind every human face."[2] When we deny the presence of God, of love and truth in another human being, we are committing violence. We are forgetting or ignoring who we are and what we are about. All of us forget who we are at various moments in our lives and so we all commit violence. The struggle of life is not to accept and legitimize our forgetfulness, our violence, but to repent of it and overcome it by doing good, by actively loving others.

When we forget who we are, we commit violence which results in physical injury and death to others, usually the destitute and voiceless poor of the third world. When we commit these acts of violence, when we deviate from love and truth, we do not know what we are doing.

The violence that happens when we forget or ignore our basic identities can take various forms on a continuum of violence, depending on the extent to which we have forgotten or ignored our basic identity. This spectrum includes any use of emotional, psychological, personal, communal or international manipulation or domination by one's will over and against another's will. Violence can take the form, on one end of the spectrum, of hatred and lying which we hold in our hearts and publicly deny and, on the other end, can include the use of physical force or power to damage or destroy humanity. It can come under the form of a spirit which makes people do what they do not want to do: threaten and inflict physical harm or any other form of punishment on others. Our support of the unjust, judgmental values of society which have led us into a nuclear arms race and militarism, and force the majority of the world into poverty, starvation, disease, homelessness, the denial of human dignity, and other injustices, is a participation in violence and a legitimization of violence. The systematic wickedness of good people in society who use cultural structures such as educational and religious institutions to defend their ideas and possessions, or who continue to work for money-making, military institutions and factories, legitimates violence. Destitution and poverty which result in early and unjust deaths among the world's poor are caused by the greed and selfishness of people who are too afraid to risk a break with the way of violence and who forget or ignore the fact that every participation in so called legitimate, systemic violence has a harmful consequence somewhere down the line on others. Our greed causes direct physical harm and death to the world's poor and thus each large and small act of greed can harm others.

Violence in society and in one's heart is a false peace, an absence of love, life and real truth, and is usually founded on self-hatred, fear and lies. It kills one's soul when it appears to be protecting and saving one's life. Violence is the step toward spiritual death which one takes when one gives in to any suicidal temptation. It is any refusal of God's gift of life. It leads not only to the death of others, but to the fulfillment of one's own suicidal spirit.

This state of violence is a state of nothingness and meaninglessness, a denial of our identities and our existence as loved children of God, where each one of us is equal and precious in God's sight. In violence, we forget our God and act as if we have no God. When we reject love, truth, hope and God in our everyday choices, in our complicity, apathy, boredom and passivity, and in the bigger decisions of our values, employment, and lifestyles, we reject ourselves and the life we can lead as children of God. Throughout history, violence has continued to lead to nothing but unhappiness, meaninglessness, despair, hunger, war, suicide, the creation and use of nuclear weapons, the perpetuation of unjust social systems, and more violence.

The struggle to be human in today's world involves overcoming the forces of violence which attack everyone from every side. In the effort to claim our inheritance as loved children of God, we must claim our love for one another and choose life. We must remember who we are. We must recall and return to the knowledge and awareness of our identity. We do not want to forget. We do not mean to do violence. But we do forget, each one of us. Nonviolence is a way of remembering and recalling, every day of our lives, who we are and what we are about, and returning to that life whenever we forget. It is noncooperation with violence, a refusing to forget. Nonviolence is a way out of the trap of violence. Nonviolence offers a way toward the fuller life of love and community as God's children. It is a way that can help us to be one human family, the beloved community God created and longs to see live in harmony.

Session 3

The Faithful Nonviolence of Jesus

Session 3
The Faithful Nonviolence of Jesus

Agenda

○ An opening reading [1 min.]

○ Experiences or insights since the last session [10 min.]
○ Small groups [12 min.]
○ Large group [10 min.]
○ Scripture reading [2 min.]
○ The Gospel in action [5 min.]
○ Large group [15 min.]
○ Reflecting on "Loving Your Enemies" (Martin Luther King, Jr.)
   [15 min.]
○ Reflecting on this section's reading [10 min.]
○ Putting active nonviolence into practice:
   a four-step process [10 min.]
○ Four step process role-play [25 min.]

○ Conclusion [5 min.]

Supplemental Material

A. Seven principles of Christian nonviolence
B. Designing daily practices to cultivate Gospel nonviolence
C. Additional recommended readings
D. Session 3 Reading:

   "The Faithful Nonviolence of Jesus," by Nancy Schreck

Session 3
The Faithful Nonviolence of Jesus

An Opening Reading — 1 min.

How can we live in the midst of a world marked by fear, hatred and
violence, and not be destroyed by it?
When Jesus prays to [God] for his disciples
he responds to this question by saying,
"I am not asking you to remove them from the world
but to protect them from the evil one.
They do not belong to the world
any more than I belong to the world."
To live in the world without belonging to the world
summarizes the essence of the spiritual life.
The spiritual life keeps us aware that our true house
is not the house of fear,
in which the powers of hatred and violence rule,
but the house of love, where God resides.
Hardly a day passes in our lives without our experience of inner or outer
fears, anxieties, apprehensions and preoccupations.
These dark powers have pervaded every part of our world to such a degree
that we can never fully escape them.
Still it is possible not to belong to these powers,
not to build our dwelling place among them,
but to choose the house of love as our home.

> Henri Nouwen,
> *Behold the Beauty of the Lord: Praying With Icons*
> (Notre Dame, Indiana: Ave Maria Press, 1987), p. 19.

Experiences, Insights Since the Last Session -- 10 min.

*Take a few minutes to reflect together on issues or experiences which this
program has raised for the participants since the last gathering. Ask
people if they would like to volunteer to share an excerpt from their nonviolence journals.*

Small Groups — 12 min.

*Form small groups of four. Before the groups begin their reflection,
read the following:*

The persons in your group have likely experienced many different teachers in their lives. People who have made sacrifices for their benefit. People who have shown them some direction in their lives. The ones who have gone ahead of them. In our shared silence, let us be present with our own awareness of those who have given us much. Let us call to mind those who have been such a gift in our own lives. Let us remember them with gratitude. *(A moment of silence.)* ...Now, let us acknowledge each other.

Members of the small groups are then invited to reflect on the following — again, at whatever level each feels comfortable:

❍ In what way has the experience of nonviolence been a part of your spiritual journey? Have you experienced God as nonviolent? Have you experienced the presence of God in the midst of this nonviolent transformation?

Large Group — 10 min.

❍ *Ask people to reassemble in the large group and to share an experience or insight that emerged during the small group reflection.*

Scripture Reading — 2 min.

Have a member of the program read this passage:

Then he made the disciples get into the boat
and precede him to the other side...
After doing so,
he went up on the mountain by himself to pray.
When it was evening he was there [all] alone.
Meanwhile the boat,
already a few miles offshore,
was being tossed about by the waves,
for the wind was against it.
Between three a.m. and six a.m.,
he came toward them, walking on the water.
When the disciples saw him walking on the water they were terrified.
"It's a ghost," they said, and they cried out in fear.
At once [Jesus] spoke to them,
"Take courage, it is I; do not be afraid."
Peter said to him in reply,
"Lord, if it is you, command me to come to you on the water."
[And] He said, "Come."
Peter got out of the boat
and began to walk on the water toward Jesus.

But when he saw how [strong] the wind was
he became frightened;
and beginning to sink, he cried out, "Lord, save me."
Immediately Jesus stretched out his hand and caught him,
and said to him,
"O you of little faith, why did you doubt?"
After they got into the boat,
the wind died down.

Matthew 14: 22-33 (New American Bible)

The Gospel in Action — 5 min.

Either present the following or ask someone in the group to read it.

We are living in the midst of a raging storm of violence.
This storm takes many forms: economic injustice, violence against women, street violence, violence in the home. Violence at work and between differing groups. Violence between nations and against the earth. And that mysterious, undeflected rage we sometimes experience within, aimed simultaneously at the world and at ourselves.

What are we to do, faced with this hurricane of injustice and violation? We can try to pretend this storm does not exist, huddling in our tiny boats and hoping against hope that its gale-force winds will not drown us. Or we can take another step. Here is a story of one group of people who confronted this violence by getting out of their little raft of presumed safety and walking on the water.

In the early 1990s in East Los Angeles, a group of women who are members of Dolores Mission Catholic Church, were searching for a solution to the heavy toll that gang violence was taking in their neighborhood. Eight gangs were active in the parish, and gang killings and injuries were an almost daily occurrence. During a particularly violent period, the women were gathered in their prayer group, praying for a solution to this carnage.

That day, the meeting's scripture reading was the one we just heard: "Jesus Walking on the Water." As the mothers prayed, one of their number — electrified with a sudden sense of discovery and consternation — shared with the others what she saw as the parallels to their own predicament. The storm on the Sea of Galilee was the gang-warfare in the streets of Boyle Heights. Fearing for their own personal safety, they had retreated behind the locked doors of their homes like the disciples huddling together in their fragile boat. They believed that the only way they would be saved was to get securely out of the line of fire. But, like those in the boat, their paralysis ultimately did not ensure them that they would be secure; they could be killed by misdirected gunfire blasting their homes or they could be shot in broad daylight walking to the market. They were as likely to become victims as much as Jesus' first century followers were, Both groups could capsize and lose everything in the maddening storm.

"Then," the woman told the others, "Jesus appears. We, like the disciples, want him magically to solve the crisis. We cry out to him, implore him to save us. But instead, he says to us, 'Get out of the boat. Come on: get out of the boat. Leave the illusion of security behind. Get out of the boat and walk on the water. Walk on the water — enter the violence-saturated streets — and we will calm the storm together.'"

"What are you saying?" the others asked, a little edgy.

She explained that she felt they were being called to walk together in the midst of the war zone of the gangs.

The others looked at her as if she had suddenly gone mad.

Yet, after a long discussion, that night seventy women (and a few men), began a *peregrinacion* — a pilgrimage or procession — from one gang turf to the next throughout the *barrio*. When they encountered startled gang-members who were preparing for battle, the mothers invited them to pray with them. They offered them chips, salsa and soda. A guitar was produced — they were asked to join in singing the ancient songs that had come with them from Michoacan and Jalisco and Chiapas. Throughout the night, in eight war zones, the conflict was bafflingly, disorientingly interrupted. People were baffled; the gang members were disoriented.

Each night, the mothers walked and within a week there was a dramatic drop in gang-related violence. The members of the newly formed *Comite Pro Paz En El Barrio* -- Committee for Peace in the Neighborhood -- had responded to the emergency of the violence being waged in their locality by "breaking the rules of war." By nonviolently intervening and intruding, they had challenged the old script of escalating violence and retaliation and created, for a time, a new and more creative script. Theirs had been more than a physical journey through their neighborhood. Most significantly, it had been the fundamental spiritual journey from the *war zone* to the *house of love*.

By entering this zone of danger, they had created a momentary space for peace. In that space, all the parties were able to glimpse their humanness. The gang-members were able to see, many for the first time, other human beings caring about them. At the same time, the women were able to let go of their paralyzing fear and anger long enough to see the human face of members of the gangs. It is no accident that the women christened their night-time journeys "Love Walks."

But this project did more than briefly interrupt the escalating cycles of violence. By provoking a confrontation with their humanness, they unleashed a process of communication and transformation. Their activity changed the gang-members and themselves. The women listened to the deep anguish of the gang-members about the lack of jobs and about police brutality. This led them, in turn, to develop a tortilla factory, bakery, and child-care center, creating some jobs and giving the gang-members an opportunity to acquire job skills. It was also a space where conflict resolution techniques were learned, because people from different gangs worked together in these projects. The women then opened a school. And they shifted from a "Neighborhood Watch" mode — where they were the eyes and ears of the police — to a group trained to monitor and report abusive police behavior, a development that has redefined the relationship between the Los Angeles Police Department and the *barrio*.

The people in this neighborhood are the first to say that they have not achieved a utopia. There is still poverty, racism and violence. Nevertheless, they have taken an enormous step toward creating a much more human environment. They did this by risking being hunman together. Or, in terms of their founding vision, "getting out of the boat" and "walking on the water."

Large Group — 15 min.

Ask people to reflect together on the elements of Gospel nonviolence in this story:

○ What are the nonviolent dynamics at work in this story?

○ In what way does this story exhibit Jesus' Reign of God in our midst?

Reflection on "Loving Our Enemies" (Martin Luther King, Jr.) — 15 min.

Here is a synopsis of Martin Luther King, Jr.'s article entitled "Loving Your Enemies," written while in jail for committing nonviolent civil disobedience during the 1955-56 Montgomery, Alabama bus boycott. After reading aloud each section, invite people to reflect on it. Then go onto the next section.

You have heard that it was said,
"You shall love your neighbor
and hate your enemy."
But I say to you, love your enemies,
and pray for those who persecute you,
that you may be children of your heavenly [Parent]..."
Matthew 5: 43-45 (New American Bible)

1) Jesus calls us to love our enemies. How can we do this?

○ We must develop and maintain the capacity to forgive. If we can't forgive, we can't love.
○ The evil deed, while not condoned, is not a barrier to restoring relationship.
○ The evil deed never quite expresses all that the other is.
○ Love strives to see the totality of the other person — the way God sees the person.
○ We must act not to defeat the enemy but to win her or his friendship and understanding.

2) What is the meaning of love in this context?

○ Not *eros* (romantic or aesthetic love) or *philia* (reciprocal
   love; intimate affection and friendship) but *agape*.
○ *Agape is* creative, redemptive goodwill and understanding toward all.
○ An overflowing love which seeks nothing in return, *agape* is
   the love of God operating in the human heart.

3) Why should we love our enemies?

○ Returning hate for hate multiplies hate.
   This chain of violence must be broken.
○ Hate scars the soul and destroys the personality —
   both of the hated *and* the hater.
○ Hate deforms; love transforms.
○ Love is the only force capable of transforming an enemy into a friend.
○ To be children of God means to actualize our unique relationship with
   God, and this means to act lovingly toward all.

4) Is this practical?

○ "Real life" is hitting back and getting even.
   This so-called practical way has failed us.
○ King says that, finally, it is time to love.

*At the end of this discussion, read this quotation from Martin Luther
King, Jr.'s essay, "Loving Your Enemies":*

   To our most bitter opponents we say: "We shall match your
capacity to inflict suffering by our capacity to endure suffering. We
shall meet your physical force with soul force. Do to us what you will,
and we shall continue to love you. We cannot in all good conscience
obey your unjust laws, because noncooperation with evil is as much a
moral obligation as is cooperation with good. Throw us in jail, and we
shall still love you. Bomb our homes and threaten our children, and we
shall still love you. Send your hooded perpetrators of violence into our
community at the midnight hour and beat us and leave us half dead, and
we shall still love you. But be ye assured that we will wear you down
by our capacity to suffer. One day we shall win freedom, but not only
for ourselves. We shall so appeal to your heart and conscience that we
shall win you in the process, and our victory will be a double victory."

Large Group Discission of This Section's Reading:
"The Faithful Nonviolence of Jesus," by Nancy Schreck — 10 min.

Putting Active Nonviolence Into Practice: A Four-Step Process
-- 10 min.

43

In this session we will practice a technique for resolving conflicts nonviolently.   It is adapted from techniques developed by author and activist Bill Moyer while working with male batterers of women.
For information on workshops which Mr. Moyer leads on moving from controlling behavior to intimacy, you may contact him at 723 Shrader St., San Francisco, CA 94117, (415) 387-3361.
Please convey the following material or have someone in the group read it.

1. Center Ourselves

Bill Moyer suggests that when we find ourselves facing violence, injustice, or other conflicts, it is important to remain in our true selves. Otherwise, we are a prisoner of our roles, including the role where we feel justified to use violence against ourselves or others.

One way to do this is to is to experience what facilitators Maureen Gatt and Gerald Hair call our "Inner Observer," the reality within us which is contemplatively and lovingly present and watching. We are invited to return to that grounded reality and to act from that place — where we are most truly ourselves. In order to do this, we ask ourselves, "What am I feeling? What is the larger picture? Where is God in this situation?" We also take time to center ourselves and thus to decide what we should do in the situation at hand.

By anchoring ourselves in our deepest reality, we are prepared to respond -- and not simply to react -- to the conflict we are facing. We may decide to protect ourselves. We may decide to engage. In either case, we can act from that place where we are most truly who we are, and not simply from a worn out and potentially desctructive script.

2. Disclose Our True Selves --
To Ourselves and to Our Opponent

This means first discovering what I am truly feeling in the situation, and then articulating those feelings to the one with whom I am in conflict. Am I feeling anger? Is there sadness or hurt or fear underneath this anger?

Second, this involves conveying these feelings to the one with whom we are in conflict. In other words, to share our heart more than our "position" or our "arguments." We should do this not in a way that "hits" the other person, but in a way that tries to get across who we really are in this moment.

3. Receive the Truth of the Opponent

This may not be my truth, but it is theirs, and we will get nowhere until we both hear each other. It is also a way of acknowledging the other. As conflict resolution specialist Marshall Rosenberg puts it, *acknowledging* does not necessarily mean *agreeing*. We don't have to agree with their position — or the interests that lie below those positions — but we can acknowledge the other person and her or his truth.

4. Make Agreements, not Assumptions

By disclosing ourselves and listening to the other, we have a chance to discover the truth and untruth of the situation. We then have the basis for making agreements about how we are going to be with one another, rather than assumptions. Many conflicts grow out of widely differing assumptions.

These four steps can be applied at every level of conflict: from interpersonal clashes to international hostility. In each circumstance, we are challenged to create the appropriate vehicles and climates to make each of these steps happen. It isn't an easy process, but in the end it will repay us immeasurably.

Four Step Process Role-Play -- 25 min.

1. Choose someone to join you in a two-person role play. Dramatize the following situation in front of the large group: Mary and Alfred are having an argument about using their jointly owned the car. Alfred believed that he could use it all week, while Mary believed that the arrangement was that Alfred had to ask to use it every day. Finally, Alfred blows up at Mary in front of other people, accusing her of being untrustworthy. Then, Alfred catches himself, and goes through the four step process.

2. In the large group, ask people to share their reactions.

3. Then, ask people to break up into pairs. Ask them to think, for one minute, of a situation where they have experienced a similar conflict. After deciding on a situation, one of the persons explains the conflict to the other, then they choose roles in this situation and, for five minutes act it out. The goal is to move from the false self to the true self by going through the four steps. After they are finished, the couple starts over, this time working with the other person's situation.

4. Have people return to the large group and reflect together on this process.

Conclusion — 5 min.

Nonviolence Journal

○ *Offer a nonviolence journal topic for the next session:*
   Please reflect on whether Jesus' nonviolent method — turning upside down the values of the world — has been present in your life?

Readings

○ *Remind the participants to read all the material for the next session:*
1) The lesson plan for Session 4
2) The supplemental material for Session 4, and
3) The reading for Session 4: K. Louise Schmidt, "Violence against Women and Children."

Evaluation

○ *Hold a brief evaluation of this session:*
1. First, ask people to share the things that worked well, and
2. Ask them to share things that could be improved.

Closing Circle and Prayer

You may want to read one or more sections of
"C. Designing Daily Practices to Cultivate Gospel Nonviolence"
found on pages 51-53. Then you may want to end with the
following:

Spirit of God,
you are a fire of justice and nonviolence
burning through our world.
Let your flame of compassion
burn through all that blocks
our wholeness and the
wholeness of this world.

Session 3: Supplemental Material

A. <u>Seven Principles of Christian Nonviolence</u>

1. Using active nonviolence to resolve conflict is a deeply religious act.

The God of Jesus loves all creatures unconditionally and longs for our unity and wholeness. Where there is brokenness, God yearns for our healing. Where there is domination, God yearns for our equality and kinship. Where life is out of balance, God yearns for equilibrium. God calls each of us to this wholeness. God's power is alive and present in this mending wherever it takes place.

We live in the midst of a system of violence. How shall we live in such a world? Shall we flee from it? Shall we go along with its degrading destructiveness? Shall we become violent ourselves? In the face of this violence, we are invited to enflesh God's longing for a world in which both the woundedness and sacredness of every person is revered and is seen to be capable of evoking the most profound healing.

The transforming power of nonviolence begins and ends with the presence of God. It is this presence which breaks the spiral of violence. It is this presence that heals and unifies what has been separated and broken. God's love heals and replenishes us so that we may heal and replenish one another. The spirit of our unifying God is presen when conflict is resolved, when the script of violence is re-written to embrace the sacredness of all parties, and when creativity is used to break the spiral of retaliation.

The God of Love is our ultimate reality. God's love is endlessly poured out upon us, vivifying and transforming us. Aware of this, Christian nonviolence challenges the violence system's overt and covert claim that *it* is life's bottom line and that even God is subject to the logic of violence. Christian nonviolence actively resists this belief as idolatry. God is not bound by the violence system. God's love is able to break every chain, to transform every form of domination or injury, to heal every separation and fragmentation. God, not violence, is the beginning and end of all that is.

Our vocation as Christians is to respond to God's call to join in the divine dance of compassionate and nonviolent love, collaborating with God's healing power to fashion the conditions for true peace. In this spirit, we are called to a ministry of active nonviolence in our homes, in our work-places, in our churches, in the streets, in the larger world, and in our own selves. This means that nonviolence is not simply a tool or a tactic. It is a spiritual journey that, with God's love, overturns the violence system in our own lives and in the life of the world.

We are not alone in our struggle for true healing. It is the Spirit of

God who plants this longing for peace and justice in our hearts. It is the Spirit of God who is with us in the midst of conflict. It is the Spirit of God who embraces us as we seek a solution to that conflict, and who is present in our reconciliation.

To engage in active nonviolence is both an act of faith in the God of Love and a way of experiencing the God of Love.

2. Human beings are meant to love and be loved.

Our true calling is to love one another as God has loved us. When we take this seriously, we are transformed into lovers who care for all beings. In practical terms this means resisting the tendency of the violence system to divide the world into various enemy camps. A fundamental script of this system is to separate "us" from "them." We play out this script especially when we put people into two categories: those who are worthy of our love and those who are not. Often, we decide that people on one side of the ledger are "right" and the other side "wrong." Sometimes, consciously or unconsciously, we take the next step and decide that those on only one side of the line are human. Our opponent then becomes an object or a monster. Often, we project our own unacknowledged violence onto him or her.

Nonviolence takes another approach. Practitioners of nonviolence seek to become their truest selves by slowly learning to love all beings, confident that all are kin and that we are called to embody this kinship concretely, especially in the midst of our most difficult and challenging conflicts. By taking this stand, nonviolence does not condone or overlook the horror of violence. Nonviolence takes physical, verbal or emotional violence utterly seriously, and is moved to action by a keen and piercing awareness of its destructiveness. Indeed, nonviolence is committed to challenging and resisting every form of violence. Nevertheless, *it does not conclude that the opponent is absolutely and irrevocably incapable of loving or of being loved.* To love the perpetrator in this way is not a sentimental or naive emotion. It is a creative and daring act that seeks to provoke all parties to make contact with their true self, the undefiled reality of God which dwells at the center of their being. In short, their sacredness.

To love the opponent means participating in the divine love of God. This means, in part, seeing our adversary the way that God sees us. But for us to see the enemy in this way, we must first see *ourselves* the way God sees *us*. This means becoming aware of our totality. It means recognizing and acknowledging our wounds: our fears, our unchanneled anger, our greed, and the patterns which keep these preoccupations festering. These wounds often contribute to what Ernest Becker in his book, *The Denial of Death,* calls our characteriological lie: the identity or persona that we have crafted to cope with life but which, in the end, becomes a kind of armor that blocks our true selves. Our wounds are at the root of whatever false front we create and maintain. In its defensive posture, this surface self is often the source of our violence. Honestly seeing and assessing our psychological and emotional fault-lines is the prelude to their transformation.

But seeing ourselves the way God sees us goes beyond seeing our wounds. It also means seeing our sacredness *which is even deeper than our wounds*. It means making contact with the incomparable presence of God at our own core. It means glimpsing our wholeness, the great gift of the God who longs for us to experience the fullness of life. It is this sacredness which helps heal our woundedness.

Nonviolence is a process of encountering this totality in ourselves and in those with whom we struggle, including those who seem the most unlovable. By opening ourselves to these two dimensions of our lives and the lives of others — where God is present in both our woundedness and sacredness — we gradually learn that no one is expendable or disposable. Nonviolence thus becomes a creative process which invites us and our opponents to break through our armor of fear, anger and greed to make contact with our sacredness.

The greatest work of nonviolence is to create situations which free the sacredness of ourselves and our opponent. There are many examples of this, but one case may especially help sharpen the point. The U.S. Civil Rights movement in the 1960s discovered creative and dramatic ways to expose the wounds of an entire social order and, in turn, to invite millions of people to reach below those wounds of racial segregation and injustice to the sacredness of human dignity, equality, and fairness. Words alone were not able to do this. It was ordinary people, putting themselves at loving and vulnerable risk, that broke through the psychological and cultural defenses which allowed many witnesses, in the Deep South and throughout U.S. society, to make contact with the humanness and the sacredness that were being violated. From the point of view of Christian theology, this breakthrough is the freeing of God's love in all the parties, creating initiative where, before, there were only emotional and political chains.

3. Nonviolence is a way to restore balance.

Human beings are called to live in right relationship with God, one another, and the Earth. In this vision, human interactions are meant to be cooperative and reciprocal. This view does not preclude conflict. In fact, it assumes that conflict will always be part of life. What such a vision maintains, however, is that *conflict need not be waged violently*. Nonviolence is a way of addressing conflict in a way that respects the humanness and sacredness of all parties.

This is a vision of human life in balance — where human beings deal with one another justly and lovingly. Often, people resort to violence as a way to restore justice: they have been injured, and so they seek to make things right by "evening the score." Unfortunately, this action becomes the pretext for the new victim's retaliatory violence. Thus, the spiral of violence continues and widens. The situation will forever remain out of balance — with fear and anger fueling the next blow, and the next one after that — until one of the parties breaks the cycle. True balance means creating ways to stop the cycle of violence and then addressing the underlying causes which sustain that violence.

Violence is the state where things are out of balance. It is for this reason that hierarchical relationships are fundamentally violent. When one person is above another person — has power over the other — there is false relationship between them. This inequality is itself violent, and it can provoke a wide range of counter-violence from the victim of this power imbalance. Active and creative nonviolence experiments are ways to transform the structure of these relationships. But they do so without using violence or without simply reversing the power-relationship, where the oppressor becomes the oppressed. Instead, it seeks to create a level playing field, an environment of mutuality and eye-to-eye interaction.

4. Violence is not automatic. It is a choice.

We sometimes think that violent thoughts and behavior are "natural." Think, for example, about a situation where we are driving in traffic and someone cuts us off. Our negative reaction is so instantaneous that it feels spontaneous, normal, and "built-in." This "naturalness" leads us to decide that our "spontaneous" reactions are simply the way it is to be human, and so we have no control over our actions.

In fact, every time we commit a form of verbal, emotional or physical violence, we are making a choice to do so. This choice is rooted in that very first time we chose violence when we were growing up. What may seem natural to us is, in fact, the product of a process in which we have been trained through a variety of "scripts."

This choice is conditioned by our social history, our cultural patterns and myths, the presuppositions we are taught, through word and deed, by our families and environments. These are very old and predictable scripts. They are, as Bernie Bush, S.J. calls them, "well-grooved neural pathways" in our society and in our own selves. When we face situations that provoke fear, anger or greed, these mental and emotional pathways are stimulated, in a way that we think is both spontaneous and a natural response. In fact, we have been assenting to these patterns throughout our life, and we ratify and reinforce them in times of crisis.

Nonviolence is the process of unlearning these "scripts" and learning new ones. This includes seeing that we have a choice whether or not to perpetrate or accommodate violence.

5. Nonviolence is a choice for a different vision of the world.

Nonviolent action does not simply seek to modify the system of violence. Rather, it strives to embody an alternative way of being. Concretely, this new way of seeing the world means helping to create the "Beloved Community," Martin Luther King, Jr.'s term for the Reign of God. The "Beloved Community" is a world where all human beings receive dignity and justice. This process comes alive in our daily life when we "break the rules of war" in the war zones at home and abroad. Achieving this dignity and justice means creating both structural and interpersonal "zones" where all people are ensured the right to life and the means of life: food, shelter, health care, freedom, mutuality and genuine relatedness. The Spirit of God invites us to collaborate in the emergence of this Beloved Community by taking concrete steps to remove the barriers to dignity and justice.

Violence cannot achieve either dignity or justice. Violence ultimately subverts dignity and justice.

6. Nonviolence is a process of repentance and transformation.

Nonviolence calls us to make a truthful assessment of things as they are in our lives and in the life of the world. The practice of nonviolence, in its most profound sense, should be a process of acknowledging the destructiveness of which we are capable, and then constructing alternatives to it.

Christian nonviolence must reflect on this dynamic of repentance and transformation in two ways. First, if we profess and strive to live Christian nonviolence, we must repent 2000 years of Christian domination and violence. To take up a consciously nonviolent life as a Christian is to resist violence perpetrated or legitimated in the name of Christ. We celebrate the ways that the Christian tradition has experimented in nonviolence, but we must also acknowledge the violence it has committed. The most profound form of *metanoia* or conversion is to take practical steps to act in a consciously nonviolent way.

Second, if we profess and strive to live Christian nonviolence, we must repent the ways in which the term "nonviolence" has been misused to breed submission or passivity in the face of violence and domination. Rather, Christian nonviolence must demonstrate a loving and relentless resistance to patterns, policies, and structures that rob human beings of dignity and justice.

7. Christian nonviolence requires an authentic spirituality.

The greatest spiritual and religious challenge today is to create an alternative to violence. This requires a profound form of public love. But, as Dorothy Day puts it, "Love is a harsh and dreadful thing, not the thing of dreams." To love ourselves, to love our enemies, and to love God requires creativity, persistence, faithfulness, and a willingness to risk everything so the sacred can be liberated in ourselves and others. This does not require being perfect in the nonviolent life. Instead, it call us to experiment with its dynamics throughout our lives.

To be able to do this, we need to be grounded in an authentic spirituality. This spirituality invites us to cultivate reverence for God's presence in every being and on earth. It summons us to see the reality around us. It recognizes that the evil and woundedness we struggle against in the world is within us as well. It calls us to disarm ourselves and others. It invites us to respond to fear with love more than courage. It gathers us into communities, knowing that we cannot do this work alone. It asks us to be willing to offer our own life rather than take someone else's. It urges us to slow down, learn patience, resist injustice, practice forgiveness, and plant the tiny seeds of love.

Nonviolence asks us to experiment with the process of dissolving the hardened armor of fear and attachment, the fortress of the ego. We are called to become free enough to allow God to see us as we are, and to consciously bear God's gaze.

Each of us is invited to discover the prayers, rituals and practices which we can use each day to help us remain aware of this spiritual journey from fear and greed to justice and compassion.

B. Designing Daily Practices to Cultivate Gospel Nonviolence

Active nonviolence is a process of bringing us back to our truest selves. Ultimately, its techniques and strategies must draw their life from the well of sacredness. Practically speaking, this means consciously cultivating those dimensions planted by God deep within our being which bring life to ourselves, to other human beings, and to the earth and its inhabitants. Now more than ever, our spiritual disciplines must deepen us in the vision and methods of nonviolent transformation.

To this end, we are called to cultivate the spiritual dimensions of the nonviolent life on a daily basis. Here are some spiritual qualities that lie at the foundation of a spirituality of nonviolence, and some suggestions for practicing them.

Awe

Often we are so absorbed in our everyday life that we assume that this is all there is. We come to believe that the structure and horizon of the world we experience -- at home, in the work-place, and through the media -- is "reality." By making this assumption, we often miss the fact that this social reality is *constructed* -- it is a system of rules, beliefs, and motivations that shape and limit our view of life. We tend therefore to overlook the fact that life is much more mysterious and unfathomable than the systems we manufacture to navigate through the world. As theologian Karl Rahner, S.J. held, these systems are like tiny islands floating on a vast sea of mystery. When we cultivate a sense of awe for the great and irreducible mystery of our lives, we are able to see that life is more than the systems in which we live. We are also able to see that those systems can and must be transformed when they contradict or offend the great mystery of God that is our beginning and end.

One way of exploring this sense of mystery is to reflect on our encounters with other persons. On the one hand, these exchanges can be like following an agreed-upon formula. In that case, we are often like two billiard balls knocking against each other. On the other, our encounters with others can be experiences of deep communion. They can be holy moments where presence receives presence, experiences where, as phenomenologist Emmanual Levinas says in *Totality and Infinity*, there is a "flow of infinity between one another's eyes." When two subjects encounter one another in this way -- giving but not being destroyed, belonging but not "belonging to" -- they experience in a momentary but tangible way the "ground of all being," the inexhaustible mystery which creates, preserves and embraces us.

One way of cultivating this sense of awe and mystery is to take some time in a quiet place and call to mind a very important encounter you had with another person. After imagining this event in detail, consider how it happened, and then what some of its consequences were. Notice your feelings as you remember this event. Reflect on the ways that this exchange had an unpredictible quality, a sense of possibility, transcending prescribed social ritual or conventional script. Sense the mystery of the situation. Reflect on how this mystery comes in part from the way that the depth dimension of both people was shared. This depth dimension or inner mystery is that aspect of us that is not reducible to our assumptions, expectations or systems. Throughout the day, cultivate an awareness of this mystery.

Gratitude

A nonviolent stance is one of deep gratefulness for our life and for all life. It is a posture which acknowledges the source of this life. It recognizes that each one of us is on a spiritual journey and that all of our experiences -- happy or sad -- teach and transform us. It salutes all the ways we have been gifted by God, our family, our teachers, our friends.

One way of cultivating gratitude is to take some time in a quiet place and recall ten people who have given of themselves so that your life could be better. Call to mind their faces. Remember in some detail what they have done for you. Recall the ways people have lavished their time, energy and resources on you. Then consider how God has lavished God's presence on you and on your world. Cultivate this awareness throughout the day, increasingly acknowledging how our entire life, and everything that passes through it, is a gift.

Receptivity

How do we cultivate our openness to those around us? One way is to practice letting go of the ego's armor in order to receive and heal the world. Here is an exercise which you can practice in the morning before leaving for work, or at any other time of the day.

Stand up, dropping your arms to your sides. Allow your entire body to relax. Breathe in God's grace; breathe it out into the world. Then slowly raise your arms and cross them in front of your eyes. Feel yourself protected and guarded. Slowly extend your arms outward in an attitude of openness to the world. After a few moments, move them in a gesture embracing the world. Repeat several times. This ritual can be performed alone or with others.

Compassion

Active nonviolence opens us to the two fundamental dimensions of all beings: sacredness and woundedness. It teaches us to share the suffering of others, as well as their fulfillment. Active nonviolence seeks to put this form of accompaniment into practice as each opportunity arises.

One way of cultivating compassion is to imagine someone with whom you have an unresolved conflict or unresolved negative feelings. Imagine them sitting in front of you. Look into her or his eyes. Share your feelings about this conflict with this person. Then ask her or him to speak. You may want to write down the "dialogue" that unfolds between you (as Ira Progoff sugggests in *At a Journal Workshop: The Basic Text and Guide for Using the Intensive Journal Process* [New York: Dialogue House Library, 1975]). Finish this encounter by praying for one another.

Joy

The horrors of this world are often overwhelming. Though they are not to be ignored -- awe, gratitude, receptivity and compassion demand nothing less than engaging them fully -- they are not the *ultimate* reality. Active nonviolence is a spiritual path that cultivates a keen awareness that *the meaning of life is found by joining wholeheartedly in God's joy.* How do we join in this divine rejoicing? We do this by letting it flow into all parts of our existence, including our modest efforts to mend the brokenness of our world.

One way of cultivating this on a daily basis is to become quiet and to imagine God laughing. Respond in kind! Go deeply into this laughter, into its roots -- into that place where God declares that creation is good, that its inhabitants are good, that life is good.

In this spirit, let us recall the words of Julian of Norwich: "The worst has already happened -- and it has been repaired!"

C. Additional Recommended Reading For This Section

Domingos Barbe, *The Theology of Conflict* (Maryknoll, NY: Orbis Books, 1989).

James W. Douglass, Chapters 1-2, *The Nonviolent Coming of God* (Maryknoll, NY: Orbis Books, 1991), pp 1-59.

Martin Luther King, Jr., "Loving Your Enemies," A.J. Muste Memorial Institute Essay Series (no date). Available for $1.00 from the A.J. Muste Memorial Institute, 339 Lafayette St., New York, NY 10012.

Thomas Merton, "Blessed Are the Meek: The Roots of Christian Nonviolence," *The Universe Bends Toward Justice: A Reader on Christian Nonviolence in the U.S.*, edited by Angie O'Gorman (Philadelphia: New Society Publishers, 1990), pp. 195-202.

Walter Wink, Chapters 6 and 9, *Engaging the Powers: Discernment and Resistance in a World of Domination* (Minneapolis: Fortress, 1992), pp 109-137, 175-193.

Session 3 Reading:

The Faithful Nonviolence of Jesus

by Nancy Schreck

A society that lacks people of vision is a society certain of its end. Perhaps the crisis in our country, our church, our world today is a result of a lack of dreamers...to open our minds...to strengthen our hearts...and to employ new energies to change our society.

Leonardo Boff

Jesus' resistance to violence begins on the first page of the gospel and continues through to the end. It is reflected in daily activities of touching, speaking, healing, and eating, but it is first born in Jesus' vision of the reign of God. When we think of the nonviolence of Jesus we often focus on Jesus' response to situations of confrontation and violence. In this essay we will explore such situations, but I suggest that they are not the starting point. This attitude of Jesus is formed long before those confrontational situations take place. In fact, those situations occur most often as a result of his nonviolent vision and approach to life.

The starting place is Jesus' vision of and commitment to the inclusive love of God that welcomes all to the one table and creates a worldview that critiques any kind of exclusion as a form of violence. One of the radical nonviolent actions of Jesus therefore is to eat with "sinners" and "tax collectors" and all those others which the society of that time excluded. Sharing a common table is nonviolent resistance to the violence of division. In Jesus' vision, we are all part of one body held in God's all embracing love. This embrace makes each one a sister and brother and thus makes nonviolence possible. One might say therefore that nonviolence is only possible in community.

True community creates an aversion to the roots of violence which define another person as "other," that is, as outside the circle of care. True community roots out violence by dismantling the motive behind so much violence, that the other is not valued. This is what Sr. Helen Prejean was able to demonstrate in her book, *Dead Man Walking*. The person convicted of a crime as well as the victim of that crime are both members of the one body embraced by God's inclusive love. This kind of love rescues and heals the enemy from violence and hatred. In the most basic and literal way it incorporates as a member of the community the one from whom we might be experiencing violence.

If the starting place for exploring the nonviolence of Jesus is in his vision of the all embracing love of God, our reflection is furthered by his vision of universal healing. This approach to life includes hope for the basic well-being of the other. This was Jesus' deepest wish for each person he encountered. In the gospel we see him moving among so many kept outside the circle of well-being by institutional violence which claimed that healing and well-being belonged to some and not to others. Jesus always found those who had been pushed outside the circle of care and invited them back into the community through the door of healing. He taught the community that its well-being was tied to the well-being of each member.

Jesus also taught that illness is not the result or fault of personal sin. Rather, the focus should be on the sinful assertion that healing is available to some and not to others — with these "others" most often being poor people and those excluded from the one table. Jesus extends healing, holy power, to the rejected and untouchable of the world. In so doing he demonstrates that no one is outside the circle of well-being. In the life of Jesus bodily healing functions as a social metaphor for another kind of healing.

The third foundation of Jesus' nonviolence is located in his understanding of God and in his approach to worship. The kind of radical love Jesus knows in God creates an awareness that human life is not about appeasing a vengeful God, but about responding in love. *This is a spirituality purified of violence at its very roots.* God, for Jesus and for those who follow the Christian way, is assertively and polemically against death in all its forms and is for life in its fullness. The enemies of Jesus, such as the Herodians and Pharisees, may have had room in their theology for a God who would require someone to suffer and die — but this is not the God of Jesus. It follows then that Jesus' attitude toward worship is also purified of violence.

The day of worship, the Sabbath, must be in service to the human community and reflect this relationship with a loving God. It does not exclude healing when that is the need. Jesus' attitude toward the Sabbath raises a question: What kind of activity would God desire to occur in that privileged time, in a dedicated place such as the temple? What kind of activity in fact best characterizes the God we worship? Jesus stands against the violence of worship that is unconcerned about human suffering. He is also concerned about the quality of the community life of those who gather for worship: are they truly sharing the one table and seeking the well-being of all? There is in Jesus a sense of urgency about reconciliation within the community before one can properly worship. "If you bring your gift to the altar and there remember that someone has something against you... " (Mt. 5: 23-24).

Therefore, before we can explore Jesus' nonviolent response to particular situations we must first see that we are talking about a person whose life is committed to the inclusion of all at one table, the well-being of all, and the worship of a God of life, not death. This means a lifestyle built on a commitment to compassion, humility, non-retaliation, forgiveness, truth-seeking, reconciliation and love of others, including one's enemies. This grows out of giving, fasting, praying, trusting, and setting our hearts on the reign of God.

This vision of life accumulated an impressive array of enemies for Jesus. The violence he encountered was intrinsic to the society of his time and eventually became focused on him personally because of the threat he posed to the way things were arranged. What was the threat? The authorities, both religious and political, realized that they would lose their power if enough people believed and acted on what Jesus taught and lived. So resistance to Jesus grew. Throughout his life he knew that people plotted against him (Mk.3:6), that the chief priests and teachers of the law were looking for a way to kill him (Mk. 11:18), and that Herod also wanted to kill him (Lk. 13:31). He was aware of other enemies: Judas, Pilate, and the professional executioners who would mock and beat and nail him to a cross.

This is too often the place we begin to explore Jesus' nonviolent way, but it is born in a far earlier place. Nonviolence was the most natural response in the world for someone deeply committed to inclusive community. Community was the goal, nonviolence a manifestation of and a means to that goal. This commitment to inclusive community in the heart works to create nonviolence in the whole person. True community takes away the motive for violence because it is the great equalizer. The violence of racism, sexism, unequal power, and value based on ability or status finds no place in the Christian perspective.

Having a vision of the loving community does not always result in creating this reality. The victory of Jesus' love for others is won in the midst of a hostile and extremely violent world. Christ does not invite us to dream about an easy-going love in a perfect utopian society, but to build a nonviolent world in the midst of reality. A key factor in building this nonviolent world is an end to retaliatory activity in the face of physical violence, legal cases and forced conscription (Mt. 5: 39-42). Jesus obliges active non-resistance to such infringement of self-interest that is destructive of the community. This kind of response is a positive contribution to the demise of the cycle of violent actions and counter-actions. The radical call is for the person to initiate reconciliation no matter who is at fault in the breach of relationship.

While Jesus in these situations was nonviolent he was at the same time determinedly confrontational, and his confrontational performances had their consequences. He is anything but the complacent victim whose simple goodness aroused opposition from a malevolent set of demonic men, as some would like to portray him. The gospel would have us see clearly that Jesus' goodness is not something passive and private. Rather, it is a goodness that brings him to initiate challenges against certain practices of his day. He provokes and disturbs. He preaches boldly in public despite the danger.

An example of Jesus' initiative is helpful. Let us look at Jesus throwing the money-changers out of the temple. Now, this is not a story of Jesus coming into the temple and being surprised by the activity happening there and responding with a sudden burst of enthusiasm to cleanse the place of worship. Rather, this "buying and selling" activity would have been well known to Jesus. What he initiates and carries out is a carefully conceived act of disruption. By doing so Jesus teaches that compassion and wrath are not necessarily mutually exclusive.

Jesus' response to his enemies was a mixture of courage and prudence. We see that at times he dodged danger (Lk. 4:30, Jn 7:1). But when face-to-face with it he did not flinch, he maintained his dignity, protected his principles, never compromised the truth, and walked the high moral ground.

At some point Jesus began to see the imminent clash between his absolute nonviolence and the atrocious violence of the sinful world in which he lived. He spoke with the disciples of the suffering he was about to endure. His decision to go to Jerusalem marked the depth of his commitment to nonviolence because he knew that his opposition awaited him there and were openly saying that they would endanger his life. It was an act of great trust in God to go into the mouth of the dragon.

Jesus' life journey would end in Jerusalem, and the question arises: If Jesus knew of the escalation of violence against him, why did he go there? It was not to fulfill some mandate of death, but to be faithful to the divine mandate he struggled to fulfill all his life, that of overcoming those who promoted death, who cultivated its structures, whose allegiance to it is seen in their willingness to kill when it is to their advantage to do so.

The important thing to remember about Jesus is that he leaves the fate of his opponents to God. Like the tradition of the lament psalms from which Jesus comes, he knows how to acknowledge the reality of evil, resist it, and then place it in Gods hands for final resolution. In the nonviolent acceptance of death Jesus acts in a way which is healing and liberating, precisely the reverse of the murderous reign of hatred and violence he experienced. Jesus is condemned, punched, spat upon, blindfolded, hit in the face, mocked without striking back. Even in agony he did not resort to the same violence used against him. He is betrayed, denied by friends, scourged, stripped, nailed naked to the cross, yet he responds with pure nonviolence.

As Gene Sharp in the book *The Politics of Nonviolent Action* writes, "Throughout history, under a variety of political systems people in every part of the world have waged conflict and wielded undeniable power by using a very different technique of struggle — one which does not kill and destroy. That technique is nonviolent action. Although it has been known by a variety of names its basis has always been the same: the belief that the exercise of power depends on the consent of the ruled who by withdrawing that consent can control and even destroy the power of their opponent." This is what Jesus did in experiencing the crucifixion. He withdrew his consent from a society of violent arrangements.

The divine response to this violence and injustice — experienced concretely in the trial and crucifixion of Jesus — is resurrection. The reaction of God to the unjust violence unleashed on Jesus is neither anger nor revenge but *new life which proclaims the limited jurisdiction of violence and injustice*. The Spirit of Christ is then handed over to the disciples so that they might continue this reconciliation and peacemaking. The divine response to violence is the gift of a spirit of patient endurance and love, and a call to the human community to make peace.

When Jesus appears to Mary at the tomb his words to her are not to be afraid — not to be afraid of what violence can do because there is a greater peace-making power at work. This is fundamental to nonviolent resistance. Lack of fear is critical, because violence can impose its will only to the extent that it's companion, death, is feared. What Jesus teaches in his experience of crucifixion is that the key to nonviolence is the process of overcoming death by fearless love. This fearless love is grounded in a commitment to remember who we are, that is, members of one family embraced by a most loving God.

Pinchas Lapide tells the story of a rabbi who was asked, "Who is the mightiest in the country?" The rabbi responded, "He who wins the love of his enemy." She who wins the love of her enemy. It is a great honor and challenge to be invited by the savior to join in this mighty kind of love. To love in this way means we will have to avoid cowardice as much as violence. We will have to commit to radical love for one another, act with courage to assure inclusive community and the well-being of each person, and ultimately let resurrection be in God's hands.

Who Is Well Off?
The Beatitudes of Jesus and the Attitudes of a Domination Society

Who in the world is well off? Who is truly blessed? What constitutes "the good life"? The sayings of Jesus popularly known as the beatitudes express some views in sharp tension with the prevailing assumptions of his day, and of ours. The beatitudes are beautiful aesthetic expressions; but they are more than that. They are a summary of basic assumptions about what constitutes well-being, being "blessed." They continue to challenge our way of thinking and way of life.

The Attitudes of a Domination Society	*The Beatitudes of Jesus (Matthew 5: 1-16)*
1. Well off are those who have all the answers.	1. Well off are those who know their spiritual need.
2. Well off are those who can insulate themselves from any suffering.	2. Well off are those who can feel the hurts in themselves and their world.
3. Well off are those who can gain control and power over others.	3. Well off are the nonviolent who see truth and compassion as power.
4. Well off are those who hunger and thirst for accumulation of possessions.	4. Well off are those who hunger and thirst for justice.
5. Well off are those who deal harshly with offenders.	5. Well off are those who extend mercy to all.
6. Well off are those who try to please everybody.	6. Well off are those who speak and live honestly.
7. Well off are those who prevail in war.	7. Well off are those who make peace.
8. Well off are those who live comfort and avoid all controversy.	8. Well off are those who are persecuted in the cause of seeking justice.

Those who hear and live out the beatitudes of Jesus are the salt of the earth and the light of the world.   Peter Ediger

Session 4

Violence, Nonviolence and Gender

Session 4
Violence, Nonviolence and Gender

Agenda

○ Opening reading [2 min.]

○ Experiences or insights since the last session [8 min.]
○ Listening exercise [10 min.]
○ Small groups [20 min.]
○ Large group [15 min.]

○ Why a *feminist* nonviolence? [20 min.]
○ Large group reflection on this section's readings [20 min.]

○ The two hands of nonviolence [5 min.]

○ The two hands exercise [15 min.]

○ Conclusion [5 min.]

Supplemental Material

A. Additional Recommended Reading
B. Session 4 Reading:

   "Violence Against Women and Children," by K. Louise Schmidt

Session 4
Violence, Nonviolence and Gender

Opening Reading — 2 min.

Ask a participant to read this reflection:

What has drawn me most strongly to nonviolence
is its capacity for encompassing a complexity
necessarily denied by violent strategies.
By complexity I mean the sort faced by feminists
who rage against the system of male supremacy but,
at the same time, love their fathers, sons, husbands,
brothers, and male friends.
I mean the complexity which requires us
to name an underpaid working man who beats his wife
both as someone who is oppressed and as an oppressor.
Violent tactics and strategies rely on polarization and dualistic thinking and
require us to divide ourselves into the good and bad, assume neat, rigid
little categories
easily answered from the barrel of a gun.
Nonviolence allows for the complexity inherent in our struggles
and requires a reasonable acceptance of diversity
and an appreciation for our common ground.
> Pam McAllister, *You Can't Kill the Spirit:*
> *Stories of Women and Nonviolent Action*, pp. 5-6.

Experiences or Insights Since the Last Session — 8 min.

Take a few minutes to reflect together on issues or experiences which this program has raised for the participants since the last gathering. Ask people if they would like to volunteer to share an excerpt from their nonviolence journals.

Listening Exercise — 10 min.

Facilitate the following exercise:

Both speaking and listening are crucial elements of active nonviolence. In this exercise, form into groups of two composed of one woman and one man. You will have two minutes, during which time, invite the woman to say whatever she would like to the man; ask the men to simply listen. (If there are few men, invite women to express to one another what they would say if a man were present.)

After this exercise is over, ask each pair to join with another pair to form a four-person group.

Small Groups — 20 min.

Members of the small groups are invited to reflect on the following — again, at whatever level each feels comfortable:

○ What did you feel while you were doing this listening exercise?
○ What experiences have you had where violence has been related to gender?

Large Group — 15 min.

○ *Ask people to reassemble in the large group and to share, first, what it felt like during the initial speaking and listening.*

○ *Then, ask people to share an experience or insight that emerged during the small group reflection (again, at whatever level they feel comfortable).*

Why a Feminist Nonviolence? — 20 min.

Ask people in the group, one after another, to read these points:

○ Women are subject to enormous interpersonal and systemic violence. Elizabeth Schussler Fiorenza and M. Shawn Copeland write, "Violence against women and their children is all-pervasive. It is not limited to one specific class, geographical area or type of persons. Rather, it cuts across social differences and status lines. White, black, rich, poor, Asian or European, Hispanic or Anglo, urban or rural, religious and secular, professional and illiterate, young and old women face violence because of their gender." (*Violence Against Women*, Concilium Series, London: SCM Press/Maryknoll, NY: Orbis Books, 1994, p. vii.)

○ We cannot speak of violence and nonviolence without addressing the widespread emotional, verbal, physical, cultural and economic violence against women in the home, the work place, the streets, and in the wider world.

○ Individual acts of male violence against women flow from the values and structures of the domination system. The domination system maintains that there is an inherent imbalance of power between women and men.

○ Feminism is the process of understanding this structural imbalance of power and changing it.

○ Traditional nonviolence also focuses on transforming our paradigm — the social "frame of reference" or world-view by which we live. But feminism deepens this traditional nonviolence by taking seriously the violence implied in traditional gender relationships. Nonviolence cannot come into its fullness without taking the question of gender equality into account.

○ Feminism exposes the gender roles assigned by society: "the authority"; "the service-provider"; "the victim"; "the rescuer." It also reveals, as Dr. Anne Brotherton maintains, the key elements of the domination system: superiority and power over others; a society of in-groups and out-groups (we/them); and a situation where peace is defined as "control through the threat of violence."

○ Feminism is a lens through which to see how power is used, and to see the consequences of the imbalance of power. But it is also a way to transform those relationships. Part of this includes articulating, and living out, a series of feminist principles which deepen our nonviolence. Dr. Brotherton identifies these principles as:

1) The fundamental importance of experience. Experience is our primary text.

2) The goal of life is not "winning," but personal and social wholeness.

3) A process that is human is one that advances mutuality and consensus, not hierarchy.

4) We are subjects, not objects.

5) The goal of nonviolence is change, not revenge.

6) A belief that there are *alternatives* to violence and injustice.

The task of Christian feminism, Brotherton holds, is "to seek the truth with love; to speak the truth with love; and to act the truth with love." (Dr. Brotherton's comments were made during a workshop on feminism for the Sisters of the Presentation, San Francisco, January, 1996.)

Discuss these ideas in the large group.

Large Group Reflection on This Session's Reading:
"Violence Against Women and Children" (K. Louise Schmidt)

— 20 min.

Ask the participants to reflect on Schmidt's ideas about feminism and nonviolence in her article.

After this discussion, reflect on other points made by Schmidt in her book, including:

○ Violence is rooted in shame. At the center of violence is shame founded in experiences of rejection, judgment, projection, and the loss of self-respect.

○ Nonviolence transforms shame by affirming the life of every individual and the right of each of us to a dignified life. It is thus a process of healing and recovering from this deep-seated shame.

○ How can we do this? How can we be nonviolent in the manner of Albert Camus, who called us to be "neither a victim nor an executioner"? For a clue, let us look at "the two hands of nonviolence."

The Two Hands of Nonviolence — 5 min.

Read this quotation aloud.

"Barbara [Deming] wrote about the two hands of nonviolence....This visual metaphor is particularly helpful in describing the basic attitude underlying the nonviolent sensibility.

With one hand we say to an oppressor, 'Stop what you are doing. I refuse to honor the role you are choosing to play. I refuse to obey you. I refuse to cooperate with your demands. I refuse to build the walls and the bombs. I refuse to pay for the guns. With this hand I will even interfere with the wrong you are doing. I want to disrupt the easy pattern of your life.'

"But then the advocate of nonviolence raises the other hand. It is raised out-stretched — maybe with love and sympathy, maybe not — but always outstretched... With this hand we say, 'I won't let go of you or cast you out of the human race. I have faith that you can make a better choice than you are making now, and I'll be here when you're ready. Like it or not, we are part of one another.'"

-- Pam McAllister, *You Can't Kill the Spirit:*
Stories of Women and Nonviolent Action, pp. 6-7.

The Two Hands Exercise — 15 min.

Ask people to form into couples and to sit down across from each other.
Lead them through the following scenario:

❍ The two of you are opponents. One of you is named **A** and the other is **B**. *(Ask them to choose which is which.)*

❍ You have had a long and tortuous relationship. Let yourself sink into this feeling.

❍ **A** clench your fists, and move them menacingly at **B**. **B** passively sit there. Do this for a while.

❍ *(After one full minute:)* **B**, slowly move out of your passivity. Protect yourself from **A's** fists with your open palms.

❍ Now, **B**, hold your two hands in the stop gesture. *(After a few moments:)* Now, **B**, keep the right hand in its stop position, but drop your left hand, in an open and relaxed way. Have it become welcoming and even friendly to **A**.

❍ (After one minute of this, ask them to stop and to share what both the **B's** and the **A's** felt.)

❍ Then, have them reverse roles and do the exercise again.

❍ After this is completed, reassemble in the large group and share feelings and insights that came during the exercise.

Conclusion — 10 min.

Nonviolence Journal

❍ *Offer a nonviolence journal topic for the next session:*
What is the role of truth in nonviolence? Are there times in your life when you "held onto the truth" in the midst of a conflict?

Reading

❍ *Remind the participants to read all the material for the next session:*
1) The lesson plan for Session 5
2) The supplemental material for Session 5, and
3) The reading for Session 5: Shelley Douglass, "The Power of Noncooperation."

Evaluation

❍ *Hold a brief evaluation of this session:*
1. First, ask people to share the things that worked well, and
2. Ask them to share things that could be improved.

Closing Circle and Prayer

○ *Closing circle: offer a brief reflection or Barbara Deming's statement that there is a "two-fold message [communicated to the opponent] that gives nonviolent struggle its leverage: We won't be bullied; but you needn't fear us. You needn't fear us; but we won't be bullied."* (McAllister, p. 7.)

Session 4: Supplemental Material

Additional Recommended Reading

Pam McAllister, *Re-Weaving the Web of Life: Feminism and Nonviolence* (Philadelphia: New Society Publishers, 1982).

_____, *You Can't Kill the Spirit: Stories of Women and Nonviolent Action* (Philadelphia: New Society Publishers, 1988).

Elizabeth Schussler Fiorenza and Shawn Copeland, eds., *Violence Against Women* (Maryknoll, NY: Orbis Books, 1994).

Session 4 Reading:

Violence Against Women and Children

by K. Louise Schmidt

The author, a Canadian citizen, reflects on the experience of domestic violence in her country. Her analysis is, unfortunately, easily applicable to other contexts, including that of the United States.

The Sexuality of Terrorism

The history of warfare as organized violence is widely practiced. In the 1970's, the Battered Women's Movement brought to our attention that women's basic human rights were being violated in ways parallel to those in prisoner of war camps. War in our homes was becoming as apparent as war abroad. It became clear how patriarchal culture has severely injured every part of human existence — our diversity, our commonality, our spirituality, our sexuality, our families and our environment.

The list of human rights violations against women and children is unending. Amnesty International reports violations that continue to occur "in every region of the world and under every system of government."[3] Today, Canada is part of an international lobby for the United Nations Human Rights Commission to adopt by consensus a resolution identifying rape of women as a war crime in response to the 50,000 Croatian and Muslim women raped by Bosnian Serb soldiers as part of a systematic strategy of war. Dispatches from Bosnia and Herzegovina include testimonies of young girls sexually enslaved and witnesses to others being slaughtered after mass rapes.[4]

The sexuality of terrorism brings its reality into Canadian living. Our daily lives are full of images of sexuality and violence presented as the epitome of male power. Male social conditioning leaves many men tragically boxed in roles that deny them whole ranges of feelings and experiences. Women are also boxed in roles which deny their full human potential. It may not be true that women are naturally less violent than men but it is true that women are physically less violent and have been socialized to be so. Men are more socialized to be violent; women and children to accept violence.

As a gender class, women are often the target of the profound fear and hatred experienced in our human race. We lose lives to conjugal violence. In Canada during 1990, two women were killed every week by their partners. An average of thirty-five assaults take place before a woman seeks police intervention.[5] Whether the violence takes place in specialized rape camps or in Canadian homes, we are called to restore deep caring in our world.

Defense Consciousness

Restoration of human dignity in each of us requires a multitude of responses. Armed response to conflict teaches a defense consciousness that will only disappear through global disarmament. Understanding how a defense consciousness has entered our daily lives is necessary for all war to end. This is especially true for the violence occurring in our homes.

Our human awareness has been distorted by fear, addictions and faulty beliefs which create reactive responses based on defense. We develop psychological and physical weapons to guard ourselves against our fear of violence and fear of loss of control.[6] The violence in our homes is expressive of wider global symptoms of distress shaped by militaristic and divisionary thinking. In each issue of gender, race and class, we have created defenses of us/them and either/or dualities. These dualities destroy mutual strengthening of relationship in personal and political spheres of living.

Disarmament then, includes not only the external weaponry of guns and missiles. It also requires understanding and release of the internal weaponry we carry within ourselves that gives rise to violence. Becoming nonviolent requires a psychological process of looking within our hearts and becoming self-aware of our motives as well as practicing what we know to be non-harming. It is an ongoing personal deconstruction of the concept of enemy and all that contributes to adversarial behaviors in our lives. The patterns of denial, despair and defense that we may feel are necessary to survive violence, are the same that prevent us from establishing healthy relationships.

No One Is Immune

Children suffer the trauma of violence when they witness abuse of their mother or father or are victims themselves. A clear statistical analysis of child abuse is difficult to assess as only extreme cases ever come to the attention of professionals. In British Columbia, it is likely 570,000 children have witnessed violence directed toward their mother.[7] A national family survey reveals nearly 1.5 million children are severely abused and 6.9 physically abused each year in the U.S.[8] The Badgley report in 1984 claims that 53% of the female population and 31% of the male population were victims of unwanted sexual acts.[9]

Adolescent prostitutes and runaways, boys and girls, commonly come from a background of abuse. Victims of childhood abuse are at a much greater risk of becoming adult abusers. A study for Correctional Services Canada found that 75% of abusive husbands came from abusive childhoods.[10] Women that leave abusive relationships may seek safety in shelters for battered women. Shelters and transition houses across Canada are most often full and have difficulty accommodating the numbers of abused women needing refuge and counseling for themselves and their children. A minimum of 600,000 women a year require this service in Canada.[11]

The Criminal Justice System is responding more seriously but how helpful are prisons in stopping violence unless alternatives to violence and recovery circles are an integral part of the healing process for men? Only in the last five years, largely because of the courage of First Nations men breaking the silence surrounding residential abuse, are we getting a clearer picture of what boys have experienced. The picture that is getting clearer tells us that no one is immune; no authority, gender, religious group, class or culture.

Nonviolent Action

Violent behavior is often the result of the will to dominate and the obsession for more—an obsession that has taken greed and exploitation nearly as far as it can go. Competition and greed, if continued at the present pace, threatens 500,000 species of plants and animals by year 2000.[12] Whole races of people have been exterminated in the name of patriarchal commerce and nationalism. The belief in this right has despiritualized and dehumanized our co-existence. Details of abuse are shocking but listening to survivors of assault gives us the truths we need to know in order to effect change. Despair and disbelief are common emotional responses that can be transformed into powerful action if we take time to listen to one another and draw support from the deep connections that exist between us. Cynicism and negativism are easy to find and stand as important clues that the world is in need of profound healing. We are all responsible for finding ways of deconstructing the enemy camps inside and outside each of us. This can begin by acknowledging that the interdependence of all life has become a fragile web weakened by the politics of profit and militarism.

It is a great challenge to disarm psychological and physical defenses which guard this truth but it is the only way forward. Anger when directed without harm can mobilize great change. But the relief and joy that result from building nonviolence in our lives and communities can be the most motivating force behind constructive lasting change. Can we find ways to reconcile with victims and perpetrators? Are we willing to address the underlying issues of power, sexuality and spirituality which violence against women has exposed? The erosion of spirit calls us to dissolve the armor of our hearts and to exist together without enemies and the need for violence. We can refuse to further the inter-generational legacy of abuse by developing practices of collaboration based on healing and generosity.

Feminism and Nonviolence

Nonviolence

For the purposes of this [essay], nonviolence is defined as *the mutual strengthening of relationship free from forms of physical, sexual, psychological or economic oppression.* This definition is mothered by a feminist vision of a just world for all which...is woven with four central threads:

1) a non-enemy ethic that is realized first with the self
2) awakening to the profound reality that "we are all part of one another"; that we are meant to co-exist
3) the belief that our children need stories of nonviolence
4) the Buddhist desire for *bahu-syam-prajayera* or "the will to be many hearts."

You Can't Kill the Spirit

Feminism is a way of seeing the world. It analyzes systems of power and questions how we live. Feminism describes what exists and why reality is the way it is. It envisions new ways and strategizes how to create change that is beneficial to all. The description, analysis, vision and strategy of feminism may change according to one's race, nationality or class.[13] But common to all definitions of feminism is an analysis of the patriarchal system of male domination and its traditional definitions of masculinity and femininity. Feminism voices women's rejection of roles and political systems which destroy the dignity and integrity of freedom and self-respect.

Feminism supports the development of ideas and alternatives that respects the diversity and commonality of humankind. It offers a mode of democracy based on participation rather than leader-based strength. Ultimately, feminism supports the liberation of individuals and groups of people from oppression. It examines use of global resources by keeping an eye on balance and redistribution. As Charlotte Bunch explained: "A feminist vision must address what kind of living and what form of distributing resources would improve the quality of life for all people while preserving the world resources for the survival of future generations."[14]

Just as feminism is more than the absence of sexism, nonviolence is more than the absence of violence. Nonviolence means power, but not as power is commonly defined in our society. Helen Michalowski writes, "Power from a nonviolent perspective is expressed in terms of empowerment of ourselves and of others, sharing, communication, create an alternative social order which draws boundless strength from having incorporated the differences of everyone's reality."[15] Joanne Sheehan in her paper, "Nonviolence: A Feminist Vision and Strategy," defines nonviolence as, "acting on the belief that we have the power to resist power-over-us through noncompliance, exercising the power-to-be who we choose to be. We refuse to be victims, to violate our own conscience. We refuse to be passive, to ignore injustice."[16]

The collaboration of nonviolence and feminism shows how to be reconciliation to ourselves as we bring it to each other. Respect for ourselves and others is a key principle in a vision based on feminism and nonviolence. It invites both men and women to examine how patriarchy impacts on our lives, our responsibilities to resist its ways of aggression, domination, and exploitation, and to build a new politics based on transformation of violence to nonviolence.

The use of nonviolence is as old or older than recorded history. There have been numerous instances of people who have courageously and nonviolently refused complicity with injustice. In *You Can't Kill The Spirit*, Pam McAllister references 225 [examples] of nonviolent action used by women around the world in struggles for social justice. What is relatively new, however, in the history of nonviolent action is the fusion of nonviolent action with mass struggle. Organized warfare is at least 30 centuries old, but organized nonviolent action as we know it is less than one century old.

Freedom Struggles

The synthesis of mass struggle and nonviolence was developed in the freedom struggle of India and pioneered by M.K. Gandhi, who led a nation to independence through nonviolent action. In Japan, since the atomic bombing of Hiroshima and Nagasaki, Japanese Buddhists have been tireless witnesses against war. Throughout Latin America, *Servicio Paz y Justicia* is working for a liberation that includes both justice and peace. The Mothers of Plaza de Mayo in Argentina are a group of women who demonstrated peacefully over the years to show the government that their disappeared children and husbands had not been forgotten. The brutal Marcos dictatorship in the Philippines was overthrown by masses of un-armed people who simply refused to cooperate and poured out into the streets in an unprecedented 'people power' revolution. In 1989 and 1990 totalitarian governments in Eastern Europe collapsed not from military attack but from the unarmed resistance of the people. Nonviolent demonstrations for women's suffrage in the United States led to the passage of a constitutional amendment guaranteeing women the right to vote. The U.S. civil rights movement won passage of The Civil Rights Act of 1964 and the Voting Rights Act of 1965 through a variety of nonviolent methods. The labor movement and the battered women's movement provide numerous examples of successful nonviolent action. The list goes on.[17]

Nonviolent Strategy

Traditionally, nonviolence action is developed through tactical strategy. Pam McAllister has summarized three categories of nonviolent action theorist Gene Sharp outlined in his work, *The Politics of Nonviolent Action*:

"The first is nonviolent protest and persuasion. With actions we name what we think is wrong, point our fingers at it and try to help others understand. This category would include such tactics as petition-ing, picketing, demonstrating and lobbying.

The second category is nonviolent noncooperation. With these actions we deliberately fold our hands and turn our backs, refusing to participate in the wrong we have named. This category would include such tactics as boycotts, strikes and tax resistance.

The third category is nonviolent intervention. With these actions we face the wrong we have named, the wrong we have refused to aid, and we step into the way, interfere, block. This category would include such tactics as physical obstruction, blockades, civil disobedience and sit-ins.[18]

Change, Not Vengeance

Barbara Deming left a wealth of work investigating the relationship of feminism to stategical nonviolence. Deming's decades of work makes clear her belief that what is essential to human liberation was not revenge but respect for fundamental rights. Vengeance, she wrote, was not the point. Change is. What can be looked for by joining feminism and nonviolence is a healing beyond resistance and a clear understanding our profound interconnectedness, co-existence and mutuality. Emphasizing our interconnections brings hope to our children. Proof there is justice for abuses creates the retribution necessary to move onward. Fundamental to any concept of social justice is the affirmation that human rights are of primary value if peace is to be restored in our families.

We can respond to violence in many ways. Acting nonviolently means we do not seek revenge or retaliation for injustice done to ourselves and others. Instead we hold ourselves and each other accountable to peacefully change and eventually transform our relationships. Holding ourselves accountable is an engaged commitment that can range from simple to complicated acts of courage. Feminism has awakened the critical consciousness that what is most required is that we assume responsibility for our problem in each of our communities. By linking the oppressive larger political systems governing most of the world with oppressive systems dominating most families we can see where to begin with ourselves.

A Life-Saving Balance

Nonviolence springs from the uniqueness of spirit and deliberate intention in each of us to create models of loving that affirm the dignity of all citizens. To develop healing models that are inclusive we depend on the individual and local creativity of each of our communities. Our first service in a nonviolent community is to help each other heal our injuries and fears — carefully converting the seeds of divisions we carry within to an acceptance that each of us belongs in our communities.

We can work with ourselves, our families and the systems binding our lives together. We can look at the personal and political meaning of how we live our lives. We can look for ways to affirm what is truly valuable and ways to resist and eventually transform the oppression in our lives. As Deming explains,

"In nonviolent struggle, we seek to hold in mind both contradiction and commonality. We refuse to cooperate with that which is in contradiction to our deep needs; and we speak to that commonality linking us all which, if remembered, can inhibit the impulse to destroy. A nonviolent dialectic — that is the dialectic that I do think accords with feminism and that we must try to invent."[19]

This is called the two hands of nonviolence. It underlies feminist sensibility by refusing to be victims, whenever possible and refusing to be violent. The oppressed in the oppressor is not ignored. In this approach there is no other; there is no enemy. Some argue this is passive. However, in Deming's words, it can be a much more passive, much more desperate act to reply in kind — to accept as one's own the oppressor's vision that there is nothing at all to prevent us from trying to destroy one another.[20]

The partnership of feminist self-assertion and the nonviolence of mutual respect is a life-saving balance that gives us strength to challenge that which cripples our humanity and to restore that which builds community. This life saving balance — this equilibrium between self-assertion and respect for others — has evolved among animals on a physiological plane. In human beings it can be gained only on the plane of consciousness. One can, it seems, only love another as one loves oneself."[21] We are looking for a politics rooted in the spirit of love - one seemingly extinct but one we can re-vitalize in our refusal to be victims or violators.

Session 5

Gandhi and the Nonviolence of Soul-Force

Session 5
Gandhi and the
Nonviolence of Soul-Force

Agenda

○ Opening meditation [2 min.]

○ Experiences or insights since the last session [10 min.]
○ Small groups [15 min.]
○ Large group [13 min.]

○ Overview of Gandhi's life and work [10 min.]
○ Gandhi and self-rule [10 min.]
○ Reflection on this section's reading [10 min.]

○ Satyagraha: Soul-Force [10 min.]
○ The steps of Satyagraha [10 min.]
○ Role-play: hassle lines [15 min.]

○ Summarizing some of Gandhi's principles [10 min.]

○ Conclusion [5 min.]

Supplemental Material

A. Milling Exercise
B. Additional recommended reading for this session
C. Session 5 Reading:

   "The Power of Noncooperation," by Shelley Douglass

Session 5
Gandhi and the Nonviolence of Soul-Force

Opening Meditation — 2 min.

Fear and love are contradictory.
Love is reckless in giving away,
oblivious as to what it gets in return.
Love wrestles with the world as with the self
and ultimately gains mastery over all other feelings.
My daily experience...is that every problem
lends itself to solution if we are determined
to make the law of truth and non-violence the law of life.
For truth and non-violence are, to me,
faces of the same coin.
The law of love will work,
just as the law of gravitation will work,
whether we accept it or not...The more I work at this law
the more I feel the delight in life,
the delight in the scheme of this universe.
It gives me a peace and a meaning of the mysteries of nature
that I have no power to describe.

> Mohandas K. Gandhi
> "My Faith in Non-Violence."

Experiences or Insights Since the Last Session — 10 min.

Take a few minutes to reflect together on issues or experiences which this program has raised for the participants since the last gathering. Ask people if they would like to volunteer to share an excerpt from their nonviolence journals.

Small Groups — 15 min.

Members of the small groups are invited to reflect on the following (again, at whatever level that they feel comfortable):

○ Gandhian nonviolence sees God as Truth and Truth as God — what does this mean to you?

○ Can you recall a time when "the truth" led you to take a stand?

Large Group — 13 min.

○ *Ask people to share an experience or insight that emerged during the small group reflection (again, at whatever level they feel comfortable).*

Overview of Gandhi's Life and Work — 10 min.

Ask people to read these passages aloud:

○ Mohandas K. Gandhi was a key leader of the Indian nationalist movement and known in his later life as Mahatma or "Great Soul." His methods and philosophy of nonviolent confrontation, including civil disobedience, played an important role in his country reaching independence from the British Empire and influenced social movements throughout the world.

○ Gandhi was born in Porbandar, India, on October 2, 1869. The family came from the traditional caste of moneylenders and grocers. His mother was a devout Jain; nonviolence and vegetarianism are central elements of Jainism. Married at 13 by arrangement, Gandhi at 18 went to study law in London. In 1891 he was admitted to the bar, and practiced law for a while in Bombay. From 1893 to 1914, he worked for an Indian firm in South Africa. He was an unsuccessful lawyer because he was unable to speak effectively in court. His life began to change when overt racist laws against Indians became increasingly restrictive. He became a part of the movement to resist these laws. It was in the midst of these struggles that he developed a series of techniques of nonviolent resistance.

○ Returning to India in 1915, Gandhi became involved in labor organizing. Increasingly involved in political protest, he became a dominant figure in the Indian National Congress. He organized civil disobedience, fasts, protest marches, and boycotts. He was imprisoned several times; his last jail term was in 1942-44, after he called for total withdrawal of the British during the Second World War.

○ Gandhi also fought for improvement in the status of the casteless Untouchables, whom he referred to as *Harijans* ("children of God"). He worked to create closer ties between the Hindu majority and the numerous minorities of India, particularly the Muslims. As Marcus and Vonretta J. Franda write, "His greatest failure...was his inability to dissuade Indian Muslims...from creating a separate state, Pakistan. When independence was finally achieved in 1947, after negotiations in which he was a principle participant, Gandhi opposed the partition of the subcontinent with such intensity that he launched a mass movement against it. Ironically, he was assassinated in Delhi on January 30, 1948, by a Hindu...who mistakenly thought his anti-partition sentiment was both pro-Muslim and pro-Pakistan."

○ Gandhi had a profound interior life. He had a deep commitment to meditation and prayer, devoting one a day a week to silence. He took the Hindu traditions, and the Christian Beatitudes, very seriously. He believed in the sacredness within the other and within himself. He believed that the great challenge facing humanity was to awaken this awareness of this sacredness in ourselves and others. As Alain Richard puts it, "Gandhi suffered when he saw this divine reality hidden, ignored or abused."

○ At the same time, he was a clever strategist. The 1931 Salt March is a classic example. As Alain Richard points out, Gandhi organized an action in which many people could defy a minor but highly significant law: the statute prohibiting Indians from making their own salt. This law forced millions of people to buy salt from the British. Some 100,000 Indians were arrested. The success of this widespread civil disobedience campaign came from the fact that it demonstrated to millions of Indians that Britain was vulnerable. It taught them that Britain could be defied, and defied successfully.

Gandhi and Self-Rule — 10 min.

Convey the following points:

The slogan for Indian independence from Britain was "Self-Rule." Gandhi wanted "self-rule," but felt, as Dr. Myron Lunine has pointed out, that it would not signal true liberation until Indians were liberated from a host of other slaveries. During speeches, Gandhi would describe this genuine self-rule by holding his hand up and use his fingers to enumerate the steps to real freedom:

○ 1st finger: remove untouchability
○ 2nd finger: Eradicate mutual suspicion between and among religious groups
○ 3rd: End the inequality of women
○ 4th: Stop addiction to drugs and alcohol
○ 5th (the thumb): End economic dependence, develop economic independence and village self-sufficiency.
○ The wrist: nonviolent action

Ask the group:

What are the fingers on *your* hands?

Reflection on This Session's Reading:
"The Power of Non-Cooperation" (Shelley Douglass) — 10 min.

Ask people what struck them about this article.

Satyagraha: Soul-Force — 10 min.

Ask people to read these points aloud:

❍ Satyagraha was the word Gandhi used to describe his creative and relentlessly persistent technique of nonviolent resistance. It combines two Sanskrit words: "sat" (meaning "truth," "soul," or "that which is") and "agraha" (meaning "firm," "steadfast," "force," "holding onto" or "gripping"). It can thus mean "soul-force" or "truth-force," but it can also mean "holding firmly to truth." It can also mean "clinging to that which is" or "firmly holding onto reality."

❍ Satyagraha is Gandhi's term for the process of waging a struggle for justice in which we seek not to exterminate the opponent but, through agapeic love and a willingness to suffer if necessary, to create with the opponent a just resolution of conflict.

❍ As Mark Juergensmeyer says in his book *Fighting Fair: A Non-Violent Strategy for Resolving Everyday Conflicts* (San Francisco: Harper & Row, 1986), "Gandhi's approach is to redirect the focus of a fight from persons to principles... He assumed that behind any struggle between two opponents lay another clash, a more basic one: the confrontation of two positions, two world-views, two sets of principles. Every fight, to Gandhi, is a fight between differing versions of the truth."

❍ Rather than a forced victory, a legal judgment, or even a compromise, satyagraha seeks to create, as Juergensmeyer writes, a situation in which adversaries "quit fighting each other, abandon each of their narrow old positions, and hunt for a resolution sufficiently broad and generous that it can incorporate both of their positions at the same time."

❍ Why fight at all? Juergensmeyer's reading of Gandhi is that "the deeper clarity — the unearthing of [the] principles that are at issue — comes only as each side challenges the other and one's position undergoes the scrutiny that only an adversary relationship can produce." Gandhi holds that while there is only one Truth, each of us only has a piece of that truth. This truth can be discerned through conflict. Satyagraha is an "approach to conflict that encourages one to search for an alternative, a deeper harmony beneath a conflict, and to hold onto it as one struggles through a disagreement."

The Steps of Satyagraha — 10 min.

Present these points:

In his book, Dr. Juergensmeyer identifies five steps of Satyagraha:

1. Analyzing the truthful and untruthful elements of each side in a conflict
2. Putting the truthful elements from each side together in a new whole
3. Advocating for this more fully truthful position in struggling with the opponent
4. Continuing to revise one's position even as the struggle continues
5. Ending the struggle when both sides agree to occupy the same position

Nonviolent action is in the service of truth throughout this process. It is utilized to: discern the truth concerning the violence or injustice one is opposing; create the climate which would encourage real dialogue; and help move the opponent from her or his recalcitrance if a resolution is not forthcoming. It demonstrates our relentless persistence, and our willingness to face suffering without inflicting violence ourselves rather than abandoning the truth that, ultimately, is in the best interests of both parties. Often, this includes open, public and nonviolent resistance carried out in a loving and firm way.

Role-Play: Hassle Lines — 15 min.

O *In this exercise, we will try to practice this Gandhian method by using a "hassle line." Hassle lines are short, intense forms of verbal role-play which enable people to try out nonviolent responses in challenging situations. We also get a feeling of how our adversaries see our action.*

O *Have people line up in two parallel lines facing each other. Each person in one line will be in a one-on-one "hassle" with a member of the other line. Tell each side who they will play, describe the confrontation, and ask them to get deeply in their roles. Have them act out their roles for a few minutes, then stop the action and ask people from each line how they felt about the confrontation and how they dealt with it. Then switch roles.*

O *Suggested hassle line scenario: The police in an unnamed city are arresting homeless people for sleeping overnight in city parks. A group of people, sympathetic to the homeless, decide to spend the night in the park as a symbol of solidarity. When they do this, a group of people from the local neighborhood angrily confront them.*

O *Have a large group discussion about this exercise and about Gandhi's principles.*

Summarizing Some of Gandhi's Key Principles — 10 min.

Share these points and then discuss them:

○ All life is one. Those who live in harmony with this law can become powerful personal and social forces for goodness. To bring this force into our lives, he explained, we had to "shed all fear." Even, Gandhi made clear, to shed our fear of death.
○ The divine is in all beings.
○ Being human means actively loving our adversaries and to identify our own blind spots.
○ Human beings cannot be reduced to the evil they perpetuate.
○ Being human means being prepared to suffer rather than inflict suffering on others.
○ Satyagraha is a process by which our interiority — our inner decision for truth, our sacredness, the presence of God deep within us — comes to be faithfully expressed in the language of our body.
  In other words, true Satyagraha matches our body language with our truest selves. Satyagraha is not simply a mechanism for change. Rather, it is a visible and public expression of an inner unity by which our inner strength, our radiant love, our compassion, our longing for the wholeness of all beings comes to be expressed in our gestures, our words, our movements, especially in our encounter with those who oppose us.

Conclusion — 5 min.

Nonviolence Journal

○ *Offer a nonviolence journal topic for the next session:*
  Have you seen the steps of Satyagraha at work in your own life?

Readings

○ *Remind the participants to read all the material for the next session:*
1) The lesson plan for Session 6
2) The supplemental material for Session 6, and
3) The readings for Session 6:
    A. St. Francis of Assisi, "The Canticle of Brother Sun."
    B. Thomas Berry, "A Moment of Grace."

Evaluation

○ *Hold a brief evaluation of this session:*
1. First, ask people to share the things that worked well, and
2) Ask them to share things that could be improved.

Closing Circle and Prayer

O Offer two quotations from Gandhi's *All Men Are Brothers* (New York: Continuum, 1980) p. 80:

"Things undreamed of are daily being seen, the impossible is ever becoming possible. We are constantly being astonished these days at the amazing discoveries in the field of violence. But I maintain that far more undreamed of things and seemingly impossible discoveries will be made in the field of nonviolence."

"Some friends have told me that truth and nonviolence have no place in politics and worldly affairs. I do not agree...Their introduction and application in everyday life has been my experiment all along."

Session 5: Supplemental Material

Additional Recommended Reading for This Session:

Joan V. Bondurant, *Conquest of Violence: The Gandhian Philosophy of Conflict* (Princeton: Princeton University Press, 1988 [1958]), pp. 15-35.

Karen Fiore, "Was Gandhi a Feminist?" *The Acorn: Journal of the Gandhi-King Society*, vol. VIII, no. 2 (Fall 1995), pp. 23-27. Address: The Acorn, Box CB, St. Boniventure, NY 14778.

M.K. Gandhi, *Non-Violent Resistance* (New York: Schocken Books, 1961).

Mark Juergensmeyer, *Fighting Fair: A Non-Violent Strategy for Resolving Everyday Conflict* (San Francisco: Harper & Row, 1986).

Thomas Merton, "Introduction: Gandhi and the One-Eyed Giant," *Gandhi on Nonviolence*, edited by Thomas Merton (New York: New Directions, 1965), pp. 1-20.

Joe Peacock, "Catching the King's Conscience, *Nuclear Times* (June 1983), pp. 14-15.

Gene Sharp, "Gandhi's Political Significance," *Gandhi as a Political Strategist* (Boston: Porter Sargent Publishers, 1979).

Krishnalal Shridharani, *War Without Violence* (Bombay: Bharatiya Vidya Bhavan, 1962).

Richard Taylor, "With All Due Respect," *Sojourners* (May 1983), pp. 13-18.

The Power of Noncooperation

by Shelley Douglass

Shelley Douglass is a longtime peace and justice activist. The following essay was written in 1983 when she was part of the Ground Zero Center for Nonviolent Action in Washington State, which conducted a Gandhian campaign focused on the Trident nuclear submarine fleet whose Pacific base was nearby.

> *Noncooperation with evil is as much a duty as cooperation with good."*
>
> M. K. Gandhi to the people of India, 1921

Gandhi used to tell his followers that *swaraj*, home-rule for India, would come only when every Indian exercised swaraj, self-rule, in his or her own life. The dependence of India upon the British, he said, was the sum of the dependence of each Indian upon British cloth, British thought, British custom, British government. British rule continued because Indians felt powerless to remove it, and because by their actions they in fact rendered themselves powerless. Gandhi was able to bring about a nonviolent freedom struggle insofar as people were able to see the truth in this insight of his: The imposition of British rule was made possible by Indian cooperation, and could be ended by noncooperation. Indians had to learn to respect themselves, to throw off the limitations of untouchability and of their own reverse racism; Indians had to learn to govern their own desires for wealth and property; Indians had to refuse to surrender to their centuries of conditioning to caste divisions so that they could work together for freedom.

For the Gandhian movement protest was not enough. One could not stand by shouting objections as a major miscarriage of justice occurred. ...Violence did not recognize the responsibility of Indians for their own problems, and so would not change anything at the deepest level. What Gandhi called for and sometimes achieved was a struggle within each person's soul to take responsibility for the evil in which she or he was complicit, and having taken responsibility, to exercise self-control and begin to change. The Salt March to the sea and the magnificent control exhibited by demonstrating Indians grew slowly from humble roots: the scrubbing of latrines in the face of social taboo, the sharing of gold jewelry by the wealthy, living and eating together in defiance of caste regulations, wearing Indian *khadi* (homespun) to withdraw support from the British economic empire. These actions and many others were symbolic of the deep change brought about by the Gandhian movement, a change in which people acknowledged their own responsibility for the wrong they sought to change, and thus in changing themselves were able to change their situation.

When violence broke out during the freedom struggle and later during partition, it happened because that vital insight was lost for a time. People again located the source of evil outside of themselves and tried to eliminate it with force. Gandhi's fasts and teachings were then concentrated on taking responsibility for the violence he might have caused, and calling people to take steps to stop their own violence. He understood that in giving up our own responsibility for evil we also give up the possibility of changing it. Gandhi's refusal to see the British as solely responsible for the situation of India was the key to Indian independence.

I believe that Gandhi's insistence upon recognizing our cooperation with evil and withdrawing it, is essential to the struggle for social change and nuclear disarmament in which we are engaged today. So often people feel powerless to create change — the leaders of political parties, the generals, the multinational executives, and such groups and persons are held responsible for our situation, and they do not listen to the voices of the poor and the disenchanted. This is true, of course. Governments and corporations exist to hold power or make a profit, and they rarely listen to polite words of protest. If our hope for change rests upon the reasonableness of any government or economic system, then our hope is slim indeed.

The underlying fact that we tend to overlook is that while systems do not listen to people very well, they are made up of the very people to whom they do not listen. The existence of a given system depends upon the cooperation of all those who do not benefit from it and all who are hurt by it, as well as upon the smaller number of people who gain status or wealth from it. If those of us who protest the injustice of our system were instead to withdraw our support from the system, then change would begin.

There are some logical steps to be taken in recognizing our responsibility and withdrawing our complicity. First, we have to know what it is that is wrong enough to justify such a step; secondly, we need to know how we are involved in supporting it; third, how we can best withdraw our support; fourth, what do we do with the support withdrawn from the system?

Involvements with the nuclear system vary. Because Kitsap County [Wasington State] where we are living, is overwhelmingly military in its nature, the decision to noncooperate here is for many a decision to leave a job. For others it has been a decision to help distribute Ground Zero's disarmament leaflets despite military prohibitions, to criticize waste and dishonesty in the Navy itself, or simply to refuse to accept the stereotypes so prevalent now of who and what "protesters" are, and try instead to hear and share.

For people not so directly involved with the military, the most obvious connection with nuclear policy is often the payment of taxes. Refusing all or part of our taxes, or paying them under protest, is a direct way to withdraw our cooperation with the making of nuclear weapons. For some, refusal to pay taxes has meant a re-examination of their convictions and life-style. They have had to become more open to uncertainty and more reliant upon faith for security as they wait to see what action will be taken by the courts. For others, the decision to live below the taxable income level has helped them to become less dependent upon the consumer goods that we take for granted. In reducing their income level to avoid financing nuclear weapons they have also begun to move out of the consumer society that necessitates these weapons.

As people refuse to give their money to the state to finance weapons, they are able to take personal responsibility for the use of their money, channeling it to a soup kitchen, a child care center, a social change project that expresses their commitment to peace and justice. Sharing of one's substance for the good of all becomes more powerful when it is done with personal involvement.

Noncooperation may include marches, vigils and tax refusal, but it includes also an inner dimension: the refusal to allow our minds to be manipulated, our hearts to be controlled. Refusing to hate those who are identified as enemies is also noncooperation.

The discipline of nonviolence requires of us that we move into the various forms of noncooperation. We will probably move slowly, one step at a time. Each step will lead to another step; each step will be a withdrawal from support of what is wrong and at the same time a building of an alternative. Negativity is never enough. It is not enough to oppose the wrong without suggesting the right. Our religious roots can help us here, with their insistence on confronting the evil within ourselves and on our unity with all peoples.

The difficult thing about nonviolence is that it is a new kind of power to us, a new way of thinking. Even as we resist the structures in our society that separate us from others, we incorporate those structures in our own minds. Nonviolence becomes not only a process of resisting our own unloving impulses. Jesus' injunction to remove the beam from our own eye before presuming to treat our sisters' and brothers' eyes, and his direction to overcome evil with good can point our way. It is true that we resist what we understand to be evil. The system does evil. But the individual people who make up the system are people like you and me: combinations of good and evil, of strength and weakness. To hate people is to incorporate part of the evil that we resist. We must learn instead to love the people while we confront the system with our lives.

At the base of love for those caught within an evil system is the understanding that we are they: that we too are caught in the same system. Just as people in the peace movement have important insights and criticisms for people in the military, military folk have critical insights to share with us. No one person owns the truth — each one has a piece of it, as Gandhi said, and if we can put all our pieces together we may find a bigger truth. Recognizing our own complicity in an evil system means that we can take responsibility for it through noncooperation. It also means that we can confront our own failures, forgive ourselves, and from that process learn compassion. We can be honest enough to admit our own imperfections and our lack of certainty, and accept the same in other people.

Just as we do not have to hate Russian people or Chinese people, we do not have to hate those who stand against our beliefs within our own country. We can be friends. We can work together in ways acceptable to all of us: to feed the hungry, to help at a school, to plan a liturgy, to sponsor activities for our children, to encourage freedom and creativity. As we work together we can get to know each other, and when that happens we can begin to explore our feelings about disarmament with mutual acceptance. Even when we feel that the people who range themselves against us have become close-minded or unreasonable, we do not have to retaliate in kind. We can find the places in ourselves where we are close-minded and unreasonable, and understand the fear behind such feelings. We can forgive and refuse to be drawn into a cycle of hate and fear. It is possible to hold out the hope of community to all people, and to work at conflicts within our communities and neighborhoods in the same spirit that we would like to bring to international conflict.

The new power of nonviolence comes from taking responsibility: personal responsibility for our own lives, and our share of responsibility for the country and the systems in which we live. The power of nonviolence lies in facing ourselves with love and compassion while honestly confronting our own evil, and then in facing the evil of our country honestly, while confronting it with love and compassion. Nonviolence is an invitation to nurture the good, to confront the evil, and in doing so to build a new community which will bear in it the best of the old.

Session 6

Cultivating Reverence for the Earth

Session 6
Cultivating Reverence for the Earth

Agenda

❍ The prayer of St. Francis [2 min.]

❍ Experiences or insights since the last session [10 min.]

❍ St. Francis and the wolf of Gubbio [10 min.]
❍ Reflecting on this story [20 min.]
❍ St. Francis and St. Clare of Assisi [18 min.]

❍ Large group reflection on this week's reading [15 min.]
❍ Process: "The Spirituality of Nonviolence and Reverence for the Earth,"
   by Susannah Malarkey, O.P. [40 min.]

❍ Conclusion [5 min.]

Supplemental Material

A. Additional Recommended Reading
B. Session 6 Reading #1: "The Canticle of Brother Sun," by St. Francis of Assisi
C. Session 6 Reading #2: "A Moment of Grace," by Thomas Berry

Session 6

Reverence for the Earth
And the Spirituality of Nonviolence

The Prayer of St. Francis — 2 min.

Invite the group to read this prayer together:

Lord, make me an instrument of your peace;
where there is hatred, let me sow love;
where there is injury, pardon;
where there is doubt, faith;
where there is despair, hope;
where there is darkness, light;
where there is sadness, joy.

O Divine Master,
grant that I may not so much
seek to be consoled as to console;
to be understood as to understand;
to be loved as to love.
For it is in giving that we receive,
it is in pardoning that we are pardoned;
it is in dying that we are born to eternal life.

Experiences or Insights Since the Last Session — 10 min.

Take a few minutes to reflect together on issues or experiences which this program has raised for the participants since the last gathering. Ask people if they would like to volunteer to share an excerpt from their nonviolence journals.

The Wolf of Gubbio — 10 min.

Arrange a dramatic re-enactment of the story of St. Francis's encounter with the wolf described in this session's reading ("How St. Francis Tamed the Very Fierce Wolf of Gubbio"). Before the session begins, choose one person to play Francis and another to play the wolf. If you haven't a wolf mask available, you could make a very simple one with card stock and a piece of string. Arrange with the actors to come into the room on cue as you read the story. Invite the rest of the participants to be the townspeople of Gubbio — have them move the chairs so as to form the "wall of the city." Narrate the following:

St. Francis and the Wolf of Gubbio

At a time when St. Francis was staying in the town of Gubbio, something wonderful and worthy of lasting fame happened.

For there appeared in the territory of that city a fearfully large and fierce wolf which was so rabid with hunger that it devoured not only animals but even human beings. All the people in the town considered it such a great scourge and terror — because it often came near town — that they took weapons with them when they went into the country, as if they were going to war. But even with their weapons they were not able to escape the sharp teeth and raging hunger of the wolf when they were so unfortunate as to meet it. Consequently everyone in the town was so terrified that hardly anyone dared go outside the city gate.

...while the Saint was there at that time, he had pity on the people and decided to go out to meet the wolf. But on hearing this the citizens said to him: "Look out, Brother Francis. Don't go outside the gate, because the wolf which has already devoured many people will certainly attack you and kill you!"

But St. Francis placed his hope in the Lord Jesus Christ who is master of all creatures. Protected not by a shield nor helmet, but arming himself with the Sign of the Cross, he bravely went out of the town with his companion, putting all his faith in the Lord.... So with his very great faith St. Francis bravely went out to meet the wolf.

Some peasants accompanied him a little way, but soon they said to him: "We don't want to go any farther because that wolf is very fierce and we might get hurt."

When he heard them say this, St. Francis answered: "Just stay here. But I am going on to where the wolf lives."

Then, in the sight of many people who had come out and climbed onto places to see this wonderful event, the fierce wolf came running with its mouth open toward St. Francis and his companion.

The Saint made the Sign of the Cross toward it. And the power of God, proceeding as much from himself as from his companion, checked the wolf and made it slow down and close its cruel mouth.

Then, calling to it, St. Francis said: "Come to me, Brother Wolf. In the name of Christ, I order you not to hurt me or anyone."

It is marvelous to relate that as soon as he had made the Sign of the Cross, the wolf closed its terrible jaws and stopped running, and as soon as he gave it that order, it lowered its head and lay down at the Saint's feet, as though it had become a lamb.

And St. Francis said to it as it lay in front of him: "Brother Wolf, you have done great harm in this region, and you have committed horrible crimes by destroying God's creatures without any mercy. You have been destroying not only irrational animals, but you even have the more detestable brazenness to kill and devour human beings made in the image of God. You therefore deserve to be put to death just like the worst robber and murderer. Consequently everyone is right in crying out against you and complaining, and this whole town is your enemy. But, Brother Wolf, I want to make peace between you and them, so that they will not be harmed by you any more, and after they have forgiven you all your past crimes, neither [human beings] nor dogs will pursue you any more."

The wolf showed by moving its body and tail and ears and by nodding its head that it willingly accepted what the Saint had said and would observe it.

So St. Francis spoke again: "Brother Wolf, since you are willing to make and keep this peace pact, I promise you that I will have the people of this town give you food every day as long as you live, so that you will never again suffer from hunger, for I know that whatever evil you have been doing was done because of the urge of hunger. But, my Brother Wolf, since I am obtaining such a favor for you, I want you to promise me that you will never hurt any animal or [human being]. Will you promise me that?"

The wolf gave a clear sign, by nodding its head, that it promised to do what the Saint asked.

And St. Francis said: "Brother Wolf, I want you to give me a pledge so that I can confidently believe what you promise."

And as St. Francis held out his hand to receive the pledge, the wolf also raised its front paw and meekly put it in St. Francis' hand as a sign that it was giving its pledge.

Then St. Francis said: "Brother Wolf, I order you, in the name of the Lord Jesus Christ, to come with me now, without fear, into the town to make this peace pact in the name of the Lord."

And the wolf immediately began to walk along beside St. Francis, just like a very gentle lamb. When the people saw this, they were greatly amazed, and the news spread quickly throughout the whole town, so that all of them, men as well as women, great and small, assembled on the market place, because St. Francis was there with the wolf.

So when a very large crowd had gathered, St. Francis gave them a wonderful sermon...and [then] he added: "Listen, dear people. Brother Wolf...has promised me and has given me a pledge that he will make peace with you and will never hurt you if you promise also to feed him every day. And I pledge myself as bonds[person] for Brother Wolf that he will faithfully keep this peace pact."

Then all the people who were assembled there promised in a loud voice to feed the wolf regularly.

And St. Francis said to the wolf before them all: "And you, Brother Wolf, do you promise to keep the pact, that is, not to hurt any animal or human being?"

The wolf knelt down and bowed its head, and by twisting its body and wagging its tail and ears it clearly showed to everyone that it would keep the pact as it had promised.

...From that day, the wolf and the people kept the pact which St. Francis made. The wolf lived two years more, and it went from door to door for food. It hurt no one, and no one hurt it. The people fed it courteously.

And it is a striking fact that not a single dog ever barked at it!

Reflecting on This Story -- 20 min.

After the play, ask people to go through the story phase by phase to see the nonviolent dynamic of the story. Ask them to discuss what happens in each phase:

◯ The experience of violence

* Wolf symbolizes the great terror and destructiveness of our lives
* There are some indications that it was a metaphor for human invaders

◯ The town's emotional reaction to that violence

* Terror
* Walled-in
* Projecting absolute evil on the wolf
* A war mentality ("they took weapons with them when they went into the country, as if they were going to war")

◯ The appeal to St. Francis for help

* No doubt, they wanted him to perform a miraculous killing of the wolf

◯ His decision to go meet the wolf

* He leaves the presumed zone of protection
* He goes without armor or weapons. The town is terrified; Francis is not afraid

◯ His encounter with the wolf

* Sign of the Cross: declaring that, even here, in this place of violence, God is present and that this is holy ground
* Calls him "Brother" — thus declaring their relatedness (and thus not an irredeemable enemy)
* Recounts the damage that the wolf has done — in other words, he speaks the truth and does not smooth over these violent acts
* Sees the roots of the problem (hunger, not malice)
* Offers to negotiate a resolution — and to be the wolf's bondsperson, that is to vouch for the wolf and to be held responsible if the wolf reneges.
* The sign of peace

○ **Francis' negotiation of peace between the town and wolf**

    * The town: afraid and probably angry when Francis brings the wolf into Gubbio, breaching the "security zone."

    * Striking the deal; restoring harmony.

○ **This is a story of nonviolent intervention**

    * Francis symbolizes how to intervene nonviolently in order to break the cycle of violence and to restore "right relationship."

Finally, ask the group what this parable tells us about the dynamics of nonviolence -- and ask them to reflect on contemporary versions of this story.

St. Francis and St. Clare of Assisi — 18 min.

Ask people one at a time to read this overview aloud in sections:

St. Francis (1181-1226) and St. Clare (1193-1253) lived at a time of dramatic economic change in Italy and throughout Europe. Feudal society was giving way to a mercantile culture marked by increasing stratification and class differences. As Louis Vitale points out, the families of the two saints represented two central aspects of the "domination system": wealth and power. Francis' family was wealthy (from accumulated capital) and Clare's family was powerful (as members of the nobility).

Francis, after his experience as a soldier (and then a prisoner of war) during a bloody and costly war, made a decision to radically transform his life. Following the model of Jesus, first Francis repudiated the reigning domination system as a form of dehumanizing slavery. He lived a life that turned those values on their head, much as Jesus did: embracing poverty, prayer and "good news" of God's beloved community, and the way of peace. It is recorded that St. Francis helped settle disputes between Italian city-states and even attempted to bring peace during one of the crusades by visiting the Sultan.

St. Clare displayed the nonviolent logic of this life in her relentlessly persistent campaign to win the "privilege of poverty" from the Vatican for her order (which originated with St. Francis and became known as the "Poor Clares"). It is also reported that she turned back an attack on the city of Assisi by holding aloft the Holy Eucharist as the invaders neared the town.

Why are peace and nonviolence so central to St. Clare and Francis? Because it is a key evangelical value and because violence is often a defense of accumulation, and thus a visible sign of one's lack of faith in and reliance on God. This nonviolence was motivated powerfully by:

○ An impassioned and empowering love of God.

○ Lives marked by great respect for the Eucharist, by fasting and prayer, and by a willingness to give their lives for this new way of the "good news."

○ "Holy Poverty" and "Lady Poverty": not destitution, but giving of oneself so that there would be more life.

○ The value of community.

○ Respecting the holiness in each person and each thing, especially those rejected by society — e.g., the poor and lepers, who were formally and legally treated as "dead" by the community.

Reflect in the large group about these ideas.

Renewing Our
Nonviolent Connection With The Earth

Large Group Reflection on this Session's Reading:
"Moments of Grace," by Thomas Berry -- 15 min.

The Spirituality of Nonviolence and Reverence for the Earth:
A Process for Reflection by Susannah Malarkey, O.P. -- 40 min.

Ask one participant to read one of the following sections, including the "points to ponder." After each section, reflect in the large group on the ideas presented there, then ask another person to read the next one.

A. Violence Toward the Earth: A Reality

A spirituality of nonviolence toward the earth must first take into account the reality of human acts of violence towards the earth as well as the connection between violation of the earth and its creatures and the oppression of the weak and vulnerable within human society. Attitudes of domination and the abuse of the vulnerable from motives of control, greed, and the arrogance of power have produced and continue to produce devastating violations of the integrity of life within both the human and the earth communities.

Points to ponder:

○ Modern humanity in its attitude of domination and disregard for the integrity of the community of life has become a threat to its own survival as well as total life on the planet.

❍ A new violence has been released over the planet within this half century. For the first time the planet has become capable of self-destruction in many of its major life systems through human agency; it has become capable of causing violent and irreversible alteration in its chemical and biological constitution. Thomas Berry, quoting Norman Myers (a specialist in the rain forests and vegetation of the world) writes, "The impending spasm of species extinction is likely to produce the greatest single setback to life's abundance and diversity since the first flickerings of life 4 billion years ago."

❍ A solution to the problems created by humanity's exploitation and abuse of nature is intimately bound up with the effort to overcome problems of social oppression and injustice. The drive of western technological society toward the domination of nature is reflected in the domination of everything presumed to be associated with it: women, people of color, indigenous people, people who work with their hands.

❍ Ideas, attitudes and values that lead to the abuse of nature are very closely related to those that cause the oppression of women, children, the poor, minorities, racial groups. The critical issue is to understand, criticize, and transform the attitudes of greed and domination in whatever context they appear.

B. The Relationship between Nonviolence Toward the Earth and Justice Within the Human Community

One cannot separate the issues of the earth's well-being and the work for peace, justice and equal access to the earth's goods within the human community. Only in the cultivation of attitudes of nonviolence and respect for the integrity of the earth community will the planet regain and maintain sufficient health to support human life.

Points to ponder:

❍ Peace, justice and the integrity of creation are profoundly inter-related. Unless ecological health is maintained, the poor and others with limited access to scarce resources cannot be fed, the sick cannot be healed.

❍ Ongoing deterioration of the environment destroys the possibilities for long term economic advance in the undeveloped world. A solution to the problems created by humanity's exploitation and abuse of nature is intimately bound up with the effort to overcome problems of social oppression, inequity, and injustice.

○ We are reshaping the earth, replacing forests with farmland, farmland with wasteland, filling rivers, lakes and seas with sediments and pollutants, unbalancing the atmosphere, subtracting species and draining gene pools, changing climate, indeed changing earth faster than it has changed ever before. We are revising creation. All this destructive effort has brought affluence to a mere fifth of the world. We are alienating the whole of nature to meet human needs, yet human needs are not being met.

C. Attitudes of Nonviolence: Right Relationship Between Humans and the Earth

False attitudes based on ignorance and prejudice can be transformed through an understanding of reality. Our violation of the natural world that results in the degradation of both the earth and the human community stems from a lack of understanding of the intimate relationship of mutual well-being within the entire life community of the planet.

Points to ponder:

○ The place of human beings on our planet is one of radical interrelation ship and interdependence with all other forms of life. We must realize that it is only by living appropriately, in proper relations with all other beings, that we can fulfill our responsibility to the whole of creation.

○ We are being warned by all indications of deterioration of the planet that unless we change our thinking and our actions immediately and radically, we may not have a planet suitable for human living to pass on to the generations that follow us. The quality of human life has already been seriously compromised by human abuse of the earth systems.

D. Change in Attitudes: Profound Respect and Sense of Responsibility For the Well-being of the Earth

A response of conscious and creative nonviolence in relationship to the earth is based on recognition of the inherent value and sacredness of all of creation. An ethic of moral responsibility springs from respect for the preservation of the gift of life, the gift of creation in all its manifestations.

Points to ponder:

○ The premise that "every form of life is unique, warranting respect, regardless of its worth to man" (from the UN World Charter for Nature) is an extension to the rest of nature of the principle of respect for the intrinsic value of each individual.

○ This world we share with each other and all other living beings on this earth is the sphere of ultimacy. There is no greater truth and no greater accountability. The only proper response is profound humility and respect.

○ In a bio-centric approach to the world, the rights of nature are defended on the grounds of the intrinsic value of animals, plants, rivers, mountains and ecosystems, rather than simply their utilitarian value to humans.

○ The moral issue of our day is whether we and other species will live, and how we will live. One has a sense of belonging to the earth, having a place in it along with all other creatures; it is our responsibility to preserve the beauty, diversity and well being of our planet earth.

○ Jesus' own teachings are especially relevant to the current critical environmental as well as social situations because they involve a direct attack on a character orientation in life that emphasizes having, domination and exploitation.

○ St. Francis of Assisi, who is widely regarded as having come as close as any mortal to realizing the perfection of Christ, came to view the sun, the moon, the earth and all living creatures as his brothers and sisters -- as fellow members of the community of God.

D. Spirituality: A Sense of the Sacred as the Basis for an Ethic of Nonviolence to the Earth

Ultimately, the depth of our attitudes and practice of respect and nonviolence toward the earth will depend on the depth of our reverence for creation, grounded in our sense of the Divine Presence at the heart of all life, as immanent within the created world. Nonviolence toward the earth community becomes an extension of our reverence for life itself. Nonviolence becomes a way of being that is truly holy because it recognizes and responds to the Sacred at the heart of life.

Points to ponder:

○ Religious concern and faith are essential to major personal and social transformation.

○ If the earth is to be saved there must be a new faith in a vision of

the good that includes environmental ethics, a faith that is
religious in nature in this broad sense.

○ A genuinely religious faith springs from the deeper center and involves
the whole personality — feeling, thought and will. In biblical language,
this deeper Center is often called the Heart.

○ Religious experience involves an encounter with the sacred and an
intuition of the awesome and wondrous mystery in the power of being.
The experience of the Sacred is of critical importance in the transformation of human attitudes toward nature and the awakening of a new
moral faith.

○ An appreciation of the miracle of life and the beauty and mystery in the
being of animals, plants and the earth as a whole must become so
intense as to generate a keen sense of the natural world's sacredness.

E. Post-Script: Wisdom from the Ancients

The eleventh century Confucian philosopher Chang Tsai writes:
"That which fills the universe I regard as my body and that which directs
the universe I regard as my nature. All people are my brothers and sisters
and all things are my companions." And in our own time, Steven
Rockefeller holds that human persons find fulfillment in this organic view
by dissolving their egoism and by living each in his or her own unique way
in harmony with the great transfo mation, adjusting to and caring for the
earth "as my body."

(The above "points to ponder" have been adapted from readings taken
from *Spirit and Nature: Why the Environment Is a Religious Issue, an
Interfaith Dialogue* edited by Steven C. Rockefeller and John C. Elder
[Beacon Press, Boston, 1992]. Thomas Berry's thoughts are adapted from
his *Dream of the Earth* [Sierra Club Books, San Francisco, 1988]. The
United Nations World Charter for Nature was adopted by the UN General
Assembly in 1982.)

Conclusion — 5 min.

Nonviolence Journal

○ *Offer a nonviolence journal topic for the next session:*

Please reflect on your relationship to the Earth. How can you live your
relationship with the environment more nonviolently?

Reading

○ *Remind the participants ro read all the material for the next session:*
1) The lesson plan for Session 7
2) The supplemental material for Session 7, and
3) The readings for Session 7:
   A) Cesar Chavez, "Letter from Delano"
   B) Bill Moyer, "Strategic Assumptions of the Movement Action Plan"
   C) Marie Dennis and Terence Miller, "The Violence of Economics."

Evaluation

○ *Hold a brief evaluation of this session:*

1. First, ask people to share the things that worked well, and
2. Ask them to share things that could be improved.

Closing Circle and Prayer

○ *Closing circle and prayer: have each person read a section of "The Canticle of Brother Sun" by St. Francis.*

Session 6: Supplemental Material

Additional Recommended Reading

Matthew Fox, "Creation-Centered Spirituality," *Cry of the Environment,* Philip Joranson and Ken Butigan, eds. (Santa Fe: Bear & Co., 1984), pp. 85-106.

Margaret Pirkl, OSF, "Our Wounded World: A Testing Ground for Exploration into Goodness," *CMSM (Conference of Major Superiors of Men) Forum* (Spring-Summer 1991), p. 23.

The Canticle of Brother Sun

by St. Francis of Assisi

Most high, all-powerful, all good, Lord!
All praise is yours, all glory, all honor and all blessing.
To you alone, Most High, do we belong.
No mortal lips are worthy to pronounce your name.
All praise be yours, my Lord,
through all that you have made,
And first my lord Brother Sun,
Who brings the light of day; and light you give to us
through him.
How beautiful is he, how radiant in all his splendor!
Of you, Most High, he bears the likeness.
All praise be yours, my Lord,
through Sister Moon and Stars;
In the heavens you have made them, bright
And precious and fair.
All praise be yours, my Lord,
through Brothers Wind and Air,
And fair and stormy, all the weather's moods,
By which you cherish all that you have made.
All praise be yours, my Lord, through Brother Fire,
Through whom you brighten up the night.
How beautiful is he! Full of power and strength.
All praise be yours, my Lord, through Sister Earth,
our mother,
Who feeds us in her sovereignty and produces
Various fruits with colored flowers and herbs.
All praise be yours, my Lord,
through those who grant pardon
For love of you; through those who endure
Sickness and trial.
Happy those who endure in peace,
By you, Most High, they will be crowned.
All praise be yours, my Lord, through Sister Death,
From whose embrace no mortal can escape.
Woe to those who die in mortal sin!
The second death can do no harm to them.
Praise and bless my Lord, and give him thanks,
and serve him with great humility.

A Moment of Grace

by Thomas Berry

We are presently, in this terminal decade of the twentieth century, experiencing a Moment of Grace. Such moments are privileged moments. The great transformations occur at this time. The future is defined in some enduring pattern of its functioning. There are cosmological and historical moments of Grace as well as religious moments of Grace.

Such a cosmological moment occurred when the star out of which our solar system was born collapsed in enormous heat scattering itself as stardust out into the vast realms of space. In the heat of this explosion the ninety-some elements were formed. Only then could the Earth take shape, life be evoked, intelligence become possible. This supernova event could be considered a Moment of Grace, a cosmological moment that established the possibilities of the entire future of the solar system, the earth, and of every form of life that would ever appear on the Earth.

Often such moments have a catastrophic aspect. For physical transformations so significant occur amid awesome violence. The world is born into a radically new phase of its existence. Another such moment occurred when newborn cellular life was imperiled by the creation of free oxygen in the atmosphere. The earlier life forms that produced oxygen could not themselves live in contact with oxygen. For while living beings as we know them cannot do without oxygen in its proper amounts, free oxygen was originally a terrible threat to every living form.

For a proper balance to be achieved and then stabilized a Moment of Grace had to occur, a moment when some living cell would invent a way of utilizing oxygen in the presence of sunlight to foster a new type of metabolic process. Photosynthesis was completed by respiration. At this moment, under threat of extinction, the living world as we know it began to flourish until it shaped the Earth anew. Daisies in the meadows, the song of the mockingbird, the graceful movement of dolphins through the sea; all these became possible at this moment. We ourselves became possible. Music and poetry and painting. All these began amid such peril.

In human history also there have been such moments. Such was the occasion in northeast Africa some 200,000 years ago when the primordial ancestor of all presently living humans began her family. Whatever talent exists in the human order, whatever genius, whatever capacity for ecstatic joy, whatever physical strength or skill; all this has come to us through this mother of us all. It was a determining moment.

There were other moments, too, in the cultural-historical order when the future was determined in some comprehensive and beneficial manner. Such a moment was experienced when humans first were able to control fire. When the first gardens were cultivated. When language was invented. Writing and the alphabet. Weaving and the shaping and firing of pottery. Then there are the moments when the great visionaries were born who gave to the peoples of the world their unique sense of the sacred, when the great revelations occurred. So too the time of the great storytellers, of Homer and Valmiki and other composers who gave to the world its great epic tales.

So now in this last decade of the twentieth century we are experiencing a Moment of Grace, but a moment in its significance different from and more threatening than any previous such moment. Now for the first time the planet is being disturbed in its geological structure and its biological functioning in a manner and to a degree unequaled in the past sixty-five million years of earth history. We are terminating the Cenozoic period in the geo-biological history of the Earth.

We are also altering the great classical civilizations as well as the indigenous tribal cultures that have dominated the spiritual and intellectual development of vast numbers of persons throughout these past five thousand years. These civilizations and cultures that have governed the sense of the sacred and established the basic norms of reality and value and designed the life disciplines of the peoples of Earth are terminating a major phase of their historical mission. Their teaching and the energy they communicate are unequal, out of their own resources, to the task of guiding and inspiring the future. We cannot function effectively without these traditions. But they alone cannot fulfill the needs of the moment. That they were not able to prevent and have not yet properly critiqued the present situation is evident. Something new has happened. A new vision and a new energy are needed.

This must arise from our new experience of the deepest mysteries of the universe that we now have through our empirical observation. We see the universe now as a developmental sequence of irreversible transformations rather than as an ever-renewing sequence of seasonal cycles. We find ourselves living not so much in a cosmos as in a cosmogenesis. If formerly we lived in a thoroughly understood sequence of seasonal change, we are now confronted with an ever-changing universe that is never quite the same, a universe of irreversible transformations. Irreversibility is now the central issue in our appreciation of where we are in the total planetary process. In the earlier context any destruction, it was thought, could be renewed as the great cycle of events enabled things to come back to their beginnings. Now we have no such assurance.

As at the moment when the amount of free oxygen in the atmosphere threatened to rise beyond its proper proportion and so to destroy all living beings, so now terrifying forces are let loose over the Earth. This time, however, the cause is from a plundering industrial economy that is disturbing the geological structure and life systems of the planet in a manner and to an extent that the earth has never known previously. The most elaborate expressions of life and grandeur and beauty that the planet has ever known are now threatened in their survival. All of this by human invention.

So severe and so irreversible is this deterioration that we might well believe those who tell us that we have only a brief period in which to reverse the devastation that is settling over the Earth. Only now has the deep pathos of the Earth situation begun to sink into our consciousness. While we might exult in our journey to the moon and the photographs showing the lunar terrain, we might also experience some foreboding lest through our plundering processes we so denude the Earth of its living forms that we be confronted with a desolate Earth that progressively is becoming more lunar in the erosion of its life forms. It is tragic to see all those wondrous life expressions imperiled so wantonly. These forms of life expression came into being during the past sixty-five million years, the Cenozoic period of Earth history, a period that might well be designated as the lyric moment of Earth expression.

In this context we must view this last decade of the twentieth century as a Moment of Grace. It is at such moments that a unique opportunity arises. For if the challenge is so absolute, the possibilities are equally comprehensive. We have finally identified the full difficulty that is before us. A renewal of planetary dimensions is underway. A comprehensive change of consciousness is coming over the human community, especially in the industrial nations of the human community. For the first time since the industrial age began we have a profound critique of its devastation and a certain withdrawal in horror at what is happening.

Much of this is new. Yet all during the prior decade studies were made that give us precise information on the situation before us. World Watch and World Resources Institute have identified in endless detail what is happening. The younger generation is growing up with greater awareness of the need for a mutually-enhancing mode of human presence on the Earth. Even in the political order we are told by a presidential candidate that concern for the environment must become "the central organizing principle of civilization."

The Universe Story is beginning to be told as a communion of subjects, not as a collection of objects. We begin to understand our human identity with all the other modes of existence that constitute with us the single universe community. In a special way all living beings of Earth are derivative from a single source. We are all cousins to each other. So too in the universe entire, every being is intimately present to and immediately influencing very other being. We see quite clearly that what happens to the non-human happens to the human. What happens to the outer world happens to the inner world. If the outer world is diminished in its grandeur then the emotional, imaginative, intellectual and spiritual life of the human is diminished or extinguished. Without the soaring birds, the great forests, the sounds and coloration of the insects, the free-flowing streams, the flowering fields, the sight of the clouds by day and the stars at night we become totally impoverished in all that makes us human.

In a corresponding manner there is now developing a profound mystique of the natural world. Beyond the technical comprehension of what is happening and the directions in which we need to change we now experience the deep mysteries of existence through the wonders of the world about us. This experience has been considerably advanced through the writings of the natural-history essayists. Our full entrancement with various natural phenomena is presented with the literary skill and interpretative depth appropriate to the subject. We experience this especially in the writings of Loren Eiseley who recovered for us in this century the full vigor of the natural history essay as this was developed in the nineteenth century by Henry Thoreau and John Muir.

There is much to be done before this last decade of the twentieth century fulfills its designation as a Moment of Grace in the actualities of the Earth story. What can be said is that the foundations have been established in almost every realm of human affairs. Finally the mythic vision has been set into place. The devastation in process now has its origin in a distorted understanding of the grand mythic vision of an emerging age of blessedness. Until this distorted dream of a technological paradise is replaced by a more viable dream of a mutually-enhancing human presence within an integral Earth community no effective healing will take place. For the dream drives the action. In the larger cultural context the dream becomes the myth which both guides and drives the action.

With this new mythic basis of a celebratory universe we can get on with our human role within that vast liturgy that is existence itself. But even as we identify this final decade of the twentieth century we must note that moments of grace are transient moments. The transformation must take place within a brief period. Such a moment may never be seen again. That in the immense story of the universe so many of these dangerous moments have been navigated successfully is some indication that the universe is for us rather than against us, that we need only to summon these forces to our support in order to succeed.

It is difficult to believe that the purposes of the universe will ultimately be thwarted although the human challenge to these purposes must never be underestimated.

Session 7

Nonviolence and Social Transformation

Session 7
Nonviolence and Social Transformation

Agenda

O Opening meditation [1 min.]

O Experiences or insights since the last session [10 min.]
O Small groups [19 min.]
O Large group [10 min.]

O Reflecting on this session's first reading [10 min.]
O Identifying social and cultural violence and injustice [10 min.]
O Role-play [15 min.]

O Key nonviolent social movements [5 min.]
O Phases of a nonviolent strategy [15 min.]
O The stages of successful social movements [15 min.]

O Reflecting on this session's second reading [5 min.]

O Conclusion [5 min.]

Supplemental Material

A. Additional Recommended Reading
B. Session 7 Reading #1: "Letter from Delano," by Cesar Chavez
C. Session 7 Reading # 2: "Strategic Assumptions of the Movement
   Action Plan," by Bill Moyer
D. Session 7 Reading #3: "The Violence of Economics,"
   by Marie Dennis and Terence Miller

Session 7
Nonviolence and Social Transformation

Opening Meditation — 1 min.

Social movements have played a central role
throughout history in achieving positive social change.
Rooted in grassroots "people power,"
nonviolent social movements
have been a powerful means
for ordinary people to act on their deepest values
and to successfully challenge
immoral and unjust social conditions and policies,
despite the determined resistance
of entrenched office power-holders.

Bill Moyer, *The Practical Strategist*

Experiences or Insights Since the Last Session — 10 min.

Take a few minutes to reflect together on issues or experiences which this program has raised for the participants since the last gathering. Ask people if they would like to volunteer to share an excerpt from their nonviolence journals.

Small Groups — 19 min.

Small groups are invited to reflect on the following (again, at whatever level each feels comfortable doing):

O What nonviolent social movement — in which you have participated or that you know about — has had the most impact on you? Please reflect on a specific experience related to this movement that was powerful and transforming.

Large Group — 10 min.

O *Ask people to share an experience or insight that emerged during the small group reflection (again, at whatever level they feel comfortable).*

Reflecting on this Session's First Reading:
"Letter from Delano," by Cesar Chavez -- 10 min.

Identifying Social Violence and Injustice — 10 min.

Please read or convey these introductory thoughts to the large group:

Nonviolent social movements emerge as a response to an injustice that violates central human and cultural values. They invite ordinary citizens to withdraw their consent from that injustice and to support a more human alternative. Unfolding in a series of stages, nonviolent social movements have made important changes in history and in our own time. Together, we will explore how nonviolent social movements work.

In the large group:

1) Brainstorm and record a list of social policies and conditions that seem to the participants to be instances of structural injustice and violence. An example is found in Session 7's Reading #3, "The Violence of Economics," by Marie Dennis and Terence Miller.

2) Take one of these examples and ask people to analyze it by:
O *Describing cases of this injustice (including one's own personal experience)*
O *Sketching the consequences of this injustice, and*
O *Reflecting on the origins or roots of this injustice.*

3) Ask:
O What social attitudes or assumptions are implied in this injustice? What social attitudes or assumptions promote or perpetuate this injustice?
O What are the myths of our culture that underlie this situation? (In this case, a "cultural myth" is defined as the fundamental beliefs by which a culture lives, not as something that is "untrue.") Examples: rugged individualism; being number one; the supremacy of competition; the primacy of consumerism; the supremacy of certain groups or communities over other ones; the "self-made man or woman"; etc.
O What are some of our positive "cultural myths"? Examples: democracy, fairness, equality, freedom. Often, these can be resources for challenging destructive myths.

Role-Play — 15 min.

Now, let's put this conflict into action. Break into small groups (four to six people). Have the group identify the different "actors" involved in this issue: who benefits, who loses; what interests support it or oppose it; what are the positions of specific corporations, governmental agencies, the media, the general public? Then, have people in the group take these different roles. Ask people to play these roles in a scenario, where one of the persons opposed to this policy has brought a proposal to change it to a negotiation session with all the other "actors."

After fifteen minutes, form the large group again and reflect together on what happened.

Key Nonviolent Social Movements — 5 min.

Ask the group to brainstorm a list of historical and contemporary social movements. Here are some examples:

- The Women's Suffrage Movement
- The Worldwide Women's Movement
- The Indian Independence Movement
- U.S. Civil Rights Movement
- The Anti-Vietnam War Movement
- The U.S. Central America Movement
- The Worldwide Anti-Nuclear Weapons Movement
- The Gay and Lesbian Liberation Movement
- The United Farmworkers Movement
- The "People Power" Movement to end the regime of Philippines President Ferdinand Marcos, 1986
- Nonviolent resistance to the Soviet coup, 1991

For an extensive chronology of nonviolent social movements, see Walter Wink, "Re-Visioning History: Nonviolence Past, Present, Future," *Engaging the the Powers: Discernment and Resistance in a World of Domination* (Minneapolis: Augsburg Fortress, 1992).

Phases of a Nonviolent Strategy: Large Group Exercise
— 15 min.

Share the following material with the group:

We need a carefully thought out strategy in order to transform social injustice and its underlying cultural assumptions. Here are some steps in this direction, based in part on *Lines of Strategy in the Nonviolent Struggle* by Alvaro Diaz (a privately published essay available from Pace e Bene) and on "M.L. King: A Way of Nonviolence." This includes:

1) Information Gathering and Analysis

In approaching any injustice that we want to transform, we need to know the facts and factors of the situation. We need to understand the

policy or condition "in the round" — from every angle.
- ○ First, this means carefully describing this policy and its consequences. Let's do that with the issue on which we have been focusing. (*Have people do this*.)
- ○ Second, this means identifying the power relations: who holds the power? We have to understand the position of the opponent and her or his interests that underlie this position. Who are the allies of the opponent? What are the cultural attitudes or assumption that keep this policy in place? In other words, how is this policy sustained? (*Have people analyze this issue from this perspective, especially looking first at the "position" — what the actors say about the issue — and then at the underlying "self-interest."*)

But this also means analyzing the power of those opposing the policy. As Gene Sharp writes in *The Politics of Nonviolent Action* (Boston: Porter Sargent, 1973), political power ultimately rests with the general population. Power is not a magical substance invested in policy-makers; in fact, policy-makers rely on the consent of the people. We need to analyze the ways the population has given its tacit or overt support to this policy. (*Have people analyze how this policy is supported. Is the support strong and vocal, or soft and tentative?*)
- ○ These steps, then, are part of the Gandhian process of identifying the truth of the situation — the truth and untruth of our position, and the truth and untruth of the opponent's position.

2) Choosing a Concrete Objective

This is based on our analysis and must address an injustice that violates central human and cultural values. (*Ask people to do this.*)

3) Dialogue

Using intelligence and persistence, communicate to the other party the list of injustices and your concrete plan for addressing and resolving these injustices. Look for what is positive in the actions and statements the opposition makes. Do not seek to humiliate the opponent but find creative ways to call forth the good in the opponent. Look for ways in which the opponent can also win. (*Have people brainstorm how this could develop.*)

4) Securing Public Support

If change does not occur, we must next secure public support for change. This involves a broad effort to educate the public, and at the same time, to build alliances with key organizations. This phase includes the development of "public participation events" (interfaith services, marches, petitions, phone-in campaigns, etc.). (*Have people brainstorm what this could include.*)

5) Direct Action

Nonviolent direct action is taken to move the opponent to work with you to resolve the injustices when the other means of persuasion have not reached the objective. These actions need to reveal with the greatest clarity the injustice being denounced. Such actions should be designed to give the largest number of people possible the opportunity to participate.

Direct action introduces a "creative tension" into the conflict. It is most effective when it illustrates the injustice it seeks to correct.

Examples can include nonviolent civil disobedience, nonviolent non-cooperation (strikes, boycotts), and nonviolent intervention (occupations, blockades). *(Have the group strategize about the direct action that should be taken.)*

6) Resolution and Reconciliation

Education, dialogue and action can create the conditions for a humane alternative to the identified injustice. This alternative addresses the specific issue at hand, and changes the dynamics between the opponents. Nonviolence seeks friendship and understanding with the opponent. Nonviolence is directed against evil systems, forces, oppressive policies, and unjust acts, not against persons. Reconciliation includes the opponent being able to "save face." Each act of genuine reconciliation is one step closer to the goal of human life, which Martin Luther King, Jr. called the "Beloved Community." Both the individuals and the entire community are empowered. With this comes new struggles for justice and a new beginning. *(Have the group consider what this might look like.)*

The Stages of Successful Social Movements
— 15 min.

Lead the group in an exploration of these eight stages:

Social movements are not spontaneous events. According to author and activist Bill Moyer, successful social movements follow eight stages. His schema helps us not only to plan social movements, it helps to overcome a sense of failure and powerlessness that we often feel — the sense that we are always losing.

We don't criticize a sophomore in college because she hasn't graduated from college; similarly, social movements are not unsuccessful just because they haven't met their objectives prematurely.

Movements build toward their goals over time, building on a series of phases.

Moyer's concept is important because it combats one of the key weapons of the status quo, which seeks to continually make its opponents feel powerless.

Apply the issue we've been discussing above to each of these stages.

For a fuller discussion, please see Bill Moyer: "The Practical Strategist," $2.00/copy, 723 Shrader St., San Francisco, CA 94117.

Eight Stages of a Successful Social Movement:

1) Normal Times

○ A critical social problem exists that violates widely held values.
○ The general public is unaware of this problem.
○ Only a few people are concerned.

2) Efforts to Change the Problem Demonstrate the Failure of Official Remedies

○ A variety of small and scattered opposition groups do research, educate others.
○ Official mechanisms are used to address the problem. This stage is a good faith effort to use the system's mechanisms for reform: hearings, the courts, the legislature. If these work, the problem is resolved. But often, when the problem is deeply entrenched, the official approaches don't work. In this phase, we go through the process of exhausting the system's official methods for correcting injustice or violence.

3) Ripening Conditions

○ Recognition by the public of the problem and its victims slowly grows.
○ Pre-existing institutions and networks (churches, peace and justice organizations) lend their support.

4) Take-Off

○ A catalytic event occurs that starkly and clearly conveys the problem to the public (e.g., the nuclear power disaster at Three Mile Island, 1979; the assassination of Archbishop Oscar Romero in El Salvador, 1980).
○ Building on the ground work of the first three stages, dramatic nonviolent actions and campaigns are launched.
○ These activities show how this problem violates widely-held values.
○ The problem is finally put on "society's agenda."
○ A new social movement rapidly takes off.

5) Movement Identity Crisis: A Sense of Failure and Powerlessness

○ Those who joined the movement when it was growing in Stage 4 expect rapid success. When this doesn't happen there is often hopelessness and burn out.

○ It seems that this is the end of the movement; in fact, *it is now that the real work begins.*
○ Virtually every successful nonviolent social movement goes through this phase. The challenge is to move through it as quickly as possible.

6) Majority Public

○ The movement deepens and broadens.
○ The movement finds ways to involve citizens and institutions from a broad perspective to address this problem.
○ Growing public opposition puts the problem on the political agenda; the political price that some power-holders have to pay to maintain their policies grows to become an untenable liability.
○ The consensus of the power-holders on this issue fractures, leading to proposals from the power-holders for change (often these proposals are for cosmetic change).
○ The majority of the public is now more concerned about the problem less concerned about the movement's proposed change.
○ Often there is a new catalytic event (re-enacting Stage 4).

7) Success

○ Majority now opposes current policies and no longer fears the alternative
○ Many power-holders split off and change positions
○ Power holders try to make minimal reforms, while the movement demands real social change
○ The movement finally achieves one or more of its demands
○ The movement needs to recognize and celebrate the successes, follow up on the demands won, raise larger issues, focus on other demands which are in various stages, and propose better alternatives and a true paradigm shift

8) Continuing the Struggle

○ Our struggle to achieve a more humane and democratic society continues indefinitely. This means defending the gains won as well as pursuing new ones.
○ Building on this success, we return to Stage 1 and struggle for the next change
○ *Key:* The long-term impact of the movement surpasses the achievement of its specific demands

See graph of these eight stages on the following page:

Eight Stages of a Successful Social Movement

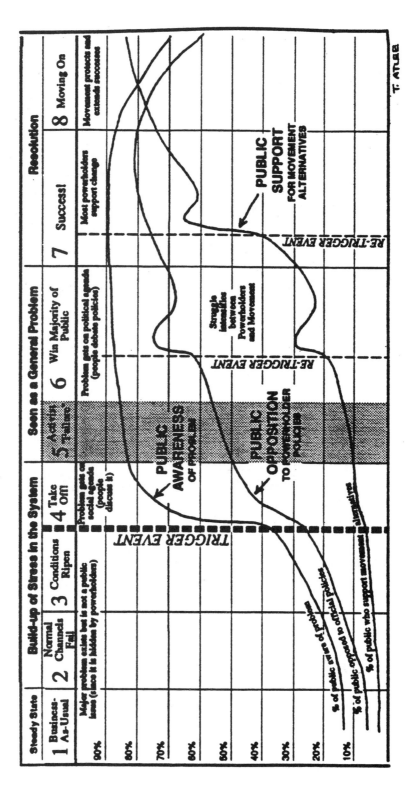

From: Bill Moyer, "The Practical Strategist"
Social Movement Empowerment Project
721 Shrader Street, San Francisco, CA 94117
Telephone: (415) 387-3361

Reflecting on this Session's Second Reading:
"Letter From Delano," by Cesar Chavez — 5 min.

Ask people to reflect on this article. How would they characterize Chavez' nonviolence?

Conclusion — 5 min.

Nonviolence Journal

○ *Offer a nonviolence journal topic for the next session:*
Please choose a social justice issue and reflect on what kind of strategy would help resolve it.

Reading

○ *Remind the participants to read all the material for the next session:*
1) The leson plan for Session 8
2) The supplemental material for Session 8, and
3) The reading for Session 8: "Fannie Lou Hamer: Baptism by Fire," by Susan Kling

Evaluation

○ *Hold a brief evaluation of this session:*
1. First, ask people to share the things that worked well, and
2. Ask them to share things that could be improved.

Closing Circle and Prayer

○ *Closing circle: Offer a brief reflection on the value of social movements.*

Additional Recommended Reading

Leonardo Boff, "Active Nonviolence and the Political and Moral Power of the Poor," Philip McManus and Gerald Schlabach, eds., *Relentless Persistence: Nonviolent Action in Latin America* (Philadelphia: New Society Publishers, 1991).

Richard Deats, "The Global Spread of Nonviolence," *Fellowship* (July/August 1996). Concise overview of recent successful sucial movements throughout the world. Reprints available from FOR, Box 271, Nyack, NY 10960. 1 copy/$1.00; 10 copies/$7.00; 100 copies/$50.00.

Bill Moyer, *The Practical Strategist (*San Francisco: Social Movement Empowerment Project, 1990), a tabloid available for $2.00 per copy from SMEP, 723 Shrader St., San Francisco, CA 94117, (415) 387-3361.

Lisa Schirch, *Keeping the Peace: Exploring Civilian Alternatives in Conflict Prevention* (Uppsala, Sweden: Life & Peace Institute, 1995).

Wilson T. Boots, "Miracle in Bolivia: Four Women Confront a Nation," in *Relentless Persistence: Nonviolent Action in Latin America,* edited by Philip McManus and Gerald Schlabach (Philadelphia: New Society Publishers, 1991), pp. 48-62.

Bill Wylie Kellerman. *Seasons of Faith and Conscience: Kairos, Confession, Liturgy* (Maryknoll, NY: Orbis Books, 1991).

Letter from Delano

by Cesar Chavez

Good Friday 1969
E.L. Barr, Jr., President, California Grape and Tree Fruit League
717 Market St., San Francisco, California

Dear Mr. Barr:

I am sad to hear about your accusations in the press that our union movement and table grape boycott have been successful because we have used violence and terror tactics. If what you say is true, I have been a failure and should withdraw from the struggle; but you are left with the awesome moral responsibility, before God and Man, to come forward with whatever information you have so that corrective action can begin at once. If for any reason you fail to come forth to substantiate your charges, then you must be held responsible for committing violence against us, albeit of the tongue. I am convinced that you as a human being did not mean what you said but rather acted hastily under pressure from the public relations firm that has been hired to try to counteract the tremendous moral force of our movement. How many times we ourselves have felt the need to lash out in anger and bitterness.

Today on Good Friday, 1969, we remember the life and the sacrifice of Martin Luther King, Jr., who gave himself totally to the nonviolent struggle for peace and justice. In his *Letter From a Birmingham Jail* Dr. King describes better than I could our hopes for the strike and boycott: "Injustice must be exposed, with all the tensions its exposure creates, to the light of human conscience and the air of national opinion before it can be cured." For our part I admit that we have seized upon every tactic and strategy consistent with the morality of our cause to expose that injustice and thus to heighten the sensitivity of the American conscience so that farmworkers will have, without bloodshed, their own union and the dignity of bargaining with their agribusiness employers. By lying about the nature of our movement, Mr. Barr, you are working against nonviolent social change. Unwittingly perhaps, you may unleash that other force which our union by discipline and deed, censure and education has sought to avoid, that panacean shortcut, that senseless violence which honors no color, class, or neighborhood.

You must understand—I must make you understand—that our membership and the hopes and aspirations of the hundreds of thousands of the poor and dispossessed that have been raised on our account are, above all, human beings, no better and no worse than any other cross-section of human society; we are not saints because we are poor, but by the same measure neither are we immoral. We are men and women who have suffered and endured much, and not only because of our abject poverty but because we have been kept poor. The colors of our skins, the languages of our cultural and native origins, the lack of formal education, the exclusion from the democratic process, the numbers of our men slain in recent wars—all these burdens generation after generation have sought to demoralize us, to break our human spirit. But God knows that we are not beasts of burden, agricultural implements or rented slaves; we are men. And mark this well, Mr. Barr, we are men locked in a death struggle against man's inhumanity to man in the industry that you represent. And this struggle itself gives meaning to our life and ennobles our dying.

As your industry has experienced, our strikers here in Delano and those who represent us throughout the world are well trained for this struggle. They have been under the gun, they have been kicked and beaten and herded by dogs, they have been cursed and ridiculed, they have been stripped and chained and jailed, they have been sprayed with the poisons used in the vineyards; but they have been taught not to lie down and die nor to flee in shame, but to resist with every ounce of human endurance and spirit. To resist not with retaliation in kind but to overcome with love and compassion, with ingenuity and creativity, with hard work and longer hours, with stamina and patient tenacity, with truth and public appeal, with friends and allies, with nobility and discipline, with politics and law, and with prayer and fasting. They were not trained in a month or even a year; after all, this new harvest season will mark our fourth full year of strike and even now we continue to plan and prepare for the years to come. Time accomplishes for the poor what money does for the rich.

This is not to pretend that we have everywhere been successful enough or that we have not made mistakes. And while we do not belittle or underestimate our adversaries—for they are the rich and the powerful and they possess the land—we are not afraid nor do we cringe from the confrontation. We welcome it! We have planned for it! We know that our cause is just, that history is a story of social revolution, and that the poor shall inherit the land.

Once again, I appeal to you as the representative of your industry and as a man. I ask you to recognize and bargain with our union before the economic pressure of the boycott and strike takes an irrevocable toll; but if not I ask you to at least sit down with us to discuss the safeguards necessary to keep our historical struggle free of violence. I make this appeal because as one of the leaders of our nonviolent movement, I know and accept my responsibility for preventing, if possible, the destruction of human life and property. For these reasons, and knowing of Gandhi's admonition that fasting is the last resort in place of the sword, during a most critical time in our movement last February 1968 I undertook a 25-day fast. I repeat to you the principle enunciated to the membership at the start of the fast: if to build our union required the deliberate taking of life, either the life of a grower or his child, or the life of a farmworker or his child, then I choose not to see the union built.

Mr. Barr, let me be painfully honest with you. You must understand these things. We advocate militant nonviolence as our means for social revolution and to achieve justice for our people, but we are not blind or deaf to the desperate and moody winds of human frustration, impatience and rage that blow among us. Gandhi himself admitted that if his only choice were cowardice or violence, he would choose violence. Men are not angels, and time and tide wait for no man. Precisely because of these powerful human emotions, we have tried to involve masses of people in their own struggle. Participation and self-determination remain the best experience of freedom, and free men instinctively prefer democratic change and even protect the rights guaranteed to seek it. Only the enslaved in despair have need of violent overthrow.

This letter does not express all that is in my heart, Mr. Barr. But if it says nothing else it says that we do not hate you or rejoice to see your industry destroyed; we hate the agribusiness system that seeks to keep us enslaved and we shall overcome and change it not by retaliation or bloodshed but by a determined nonviolent struggle carried on by those masses of farm workers who intend to be free and human.

Sincerely yours,

Cesar E. Chavez
United Farm Workers Organizing Committee, A.F.L.-C.I.O., Delano, CA

Strategic Assumptions of the Movement Action Plan

by Bill Moyer

The Movement Action Plan is an evolving set of strategic models and methods for analyzing and conducting social movements. The MAP analysis reflects a number of underlying strategic operating assumptions about social movements that have strong implications for evaluating and conducting social movements. The following are seven MAP strategic assumptions:

1. Social Movements Are Proven To Be Powerful

Social movements have been a powerful means for ordinary people to participate directly in creating positive social change, particularly when formal channels for democratic political participation do not work. Social movements helped end slavery, create labor unions and child labor laws, attain women's suffrage, end atmospheric nuclear testing, achieve many civil rights for blacks, women, gays and lesbians, end the Vietnam War, oust dictators like Marcos and Duvalier, challenge South African Apartheid, curb the cold war, and move Eastern Bloc nations toward democracy. Almost every positive aspect of American society has been influenced by successful people's movements.

Social movements are more numerous and powerful than ever. Much acclaim is given to the social movements of the 1960s, but those of the 1970s and 1980s were bigger and more numerous. The 1970s included the women's, gay and lesbian, anti-Vietnam War, United Farm Workers, and anti-nuclear energy movements. While these continued in the 1980s, many new movements emerged, such as those concerned with nuclear weapons, nonintervention in Central America, homelessness, South African apartheid, and the democratization of China, the USSR, the Eastern Bloc, the Philippines, and Haiti.

2. Movements Are At The Center of Society

Most social movements are not exceptional [or] rare protest events on society's fringe, and activists are not anti-American rebels. Quite the contrary, progressive nonviolent social movements are at the center of society's "historicity," the on-going process of society evolving and redefining itself. In the words of Dr. Martin Luther King, a chief purpose of social movements is "to fulfill the American Dream, not to destroy it." Social movements are deeply grounded in our founding values of justice, democracy, civil right, security, and freedom. In contrast, they oppose vested interests that use public offices and corporate institutions in ways that violate these principles.

Implication: Social movements, therefore, must consciously articulate society's central value and sensibilities. Almost all ordinary citizens consider themselves patriots; that is, they strongly believe in the positive values of their country. Movement activists will be successful only to the extent that they can convince the great majority of people that the movement, and not the powerholders, truly represent society's values and sensibilities. In contrast, movements are self-destructive to the extent that they define themselves as being rebels on the fringes of society who oppose the majority and are trying to overthrow core social values and structures.

3. The Real Issue Is Social Justice Vs. Vested Interest

The experience of social movements is consistent with Arnold Toynbee's dictum that the real struggle in the world is between vested interests and social justice. An elite minority holds enormous political, economic, and social power and influence, which they use to benefit a minority of elites at the expense of society's majority.

In their attempt to promote democracy, justice, peace, ecological sustainability, and the general social welfare, social movements must oppose the excessive power and influence of the elite powerholders. The consequence of such opposition is, inevitably, conflict with the political, economic, and corporate powerholders—whether they be military contractors wanting to increase the military budget and prolong the nuclear arms race, doctors wanting to undermine guaranteed health care, or logging companies wanting to destroy the remaining old-growth forests. The struggle between vested interests and social welfare will be intensified with the growing crises during in the 1990s.

Implication: In the face of this inevitable struggle, movement activists must neither become discouraged nor believe their movement is losing when powerholders do not change their minds or policies. Even though a social movement may be supported by a majority who opposes current policies and condition, powerholders will fight until it becomes in their interest to change.

4. The Grand Strategy Is To Promote Participatory Democracy

The grand strategy of social movements is to promote participatory democracy through people power, in which an ever-increasing majority of ordinary citizen is alerted, won over, and becomes involved in addressing critical social problems and achieving progressive change.

The lack of democracy is a major source of social problems. The American system increasingly exemplifies that power corrupts and absolute power corrupts absolutely. When a society functions to support the self-serving interests of its privileged few, lack of concern for the welfare of all people helps to engender environmental destruction, massive poverty, reduced social programs, vast military expenditures, support of Third World dictators, and global military intervention.

Political power ultimately rests with the general population. The official power-holders in any society can only rule as long as they have the consent of the people. Ultimately, the general population will give this consent only as long as those who govern are perceived to be upholding the public trust and the basic morals, values, and interests of the whole society. (That is why all governments — including those of the democratic West as well as the harshest dictatorships — spend enormous money and effort trying to justify their power and policies to the ordinary public, wrapping them in terms of widely-accepted values and traditions.) There have been remarkable recent examples of the power of ordinary citizens to overthrow even brutal Stalinist dictatorships in the Eastern Bloc nations....

Participatory democracy, led by social movement people-power, therefore, is a key to facing the awesome problems that confront us today and to establishing a more humane world. The resolution of today's problems require an informed, empowered and politicized population that assertively demands democracy, justice, security, equality, human welfare, peace, and ecological preservation.

5. The Target Constituency Is The Ordinary Citizen

The primary target constituency of social movements is ordinary citizens, not powerholders. Social change happens only when the majority of citizens are alerted, educated, and motivated to be concerned about a problem. Social movements are only as powerful as the power of their grassroots support. The chief task of the activist, therefore, is to focus on and to win over the public, not to change the minds and policies of official powerholders.

Implication: The formal powerholders will not change their policies until there is overwhelming pressure from the general population. Ignoring this reality is a chief source of activists' feelings of powerlessness and movement failure. When powerholders fail to respond to initial movement demands, many activists become depressed and angry. This can lead to burnout, dropout, unnecessary compromises, or aimless rebelliousness. This creates a cycle of increased failure, because rebellious acts alienate the general public, the true source of movement power.

6. Success is a Long-Term Process, Not An Event

The process of putting a social problem on society's agenda, winning a large majority, and subsequently achieving long-range movement goals (such as cutting the military budget in half and curbing the cold war) occurs over many years. This lengthy process incudes reaching many sub-goals along the way.

Implications: Activists should evaluate their movement by how well it is moving along the road of success, not by whether it has achieved its long-term goals. And activists should develop strategies and tactics that advance their movement along the next segment of the road, instead of trying to achieve the long-range goals directly—and feeling they have failed because those long-range goals have not yet been reached.

7. Social Movements Must Be Nonviolent

Following Gandhi and King, the ideology and method of nonviolence provides social movements with the optimum opportunity to win over and involve the general citizenry in people power because:

○ Nonviolence, unlike militaristic methods, allows most everyone to participate: women men, elderly, youth and even children; people from all traditional levels of strength and weakness.

○ Nonviolence is based on timeless national, cultural, human, and religious values and principles such as love, understanding, forgiveness, caring, compassion, justice, democracy, equality, security and preservation.

○ Nonviolence appeals to these values and principles held by people and nations.

○ Nonviolence is less threatening to ordinary citizens.

○ In nonviolence, the means are consistent with the ends—they are the ends in the making.

○ Nonviolence has the capacity to reduce the effectiveness of police and state violence—the powerholders' ultimate weapon — and to turn it to the movement's advantage.

○ A clear policy of nonviolence makes it difficult for *agent provocateurs* to disrupt or discredit movements by promoting internal violence, hostility, dissension, dishonesty and confusion.

○ Successful social movements need participants and organizations that effectively play four different roles: citizen, rebel, social change agent, and reformer.

The Violence of Economics

by Marie Dennis and Terence Miller

Some of the most violent confrontations in this post-modern world take place on the economic playing field, where millions of people and their communities are simply excluded from play. They are not needed as workers at home, unwelcome as migrant workers, and unable to achieve the dubious title of "consumer." In a world where value is increasingly assigned according to the form and quality of participation in economic life, an increasing number of poor people in the prosperous North and poor South are simply considered "disposable."

According to the United Nations Development Program (22), the most serious threats to human security in the post-Cold War world lies in military conflicts within nations that originate in "socio-economic deprivation and disparities." The income of the richest fifth of humanity is over sixty times that of the poorest fifth. The wealthiest twenty percent controls eighty-three percent of the world's income, while the poorest twenty percent survives on only 1.4%. Over one billion human beings eke out an existence on just $1.00 per day. Three billion human beings live on little more than $2.00. At the same time, 358 individuals have accumulated personal capital worth about $762 billion, the equivalent income of about 2.35 billion poor people.(23)

Forms of Economic Violence

Violence is the heavy burden of debt carried by many of the poorest countries. According to a recent Oxfam International report, "It would be possible by the year 2000 to make social investments which would save the lives of around 21 million African children and provide 90 million girls with access to primary education"(24) for less than is currently being spent on debt by these countries.

Violence is austerity or adjustment programs promoted by international financial institutions to "help" poor countries recover from economic crisis, especially when they only attend to macro-economic indicators without concern for human or environmental costs. No solutions to economic crises are morally tenable if they maintain or worsen human misery. For example, Tanzania "adjusted" its economy by dramatically decreasing government expenditures. Free education was ended and enrollment in primary schools fell from 90% in 1980 to 70% today. Illiteracy rates have risen by half in less than a decade.(25)

Violence is profit-driven world-wide economic integration that destroys local economies, customs, and communities. As Mexico prepared to negotiate the North American Free Trade Agreement with the United States and Canada, constitutional changes were enacted to make Mexico a more attractive trading partner. One of these dramatically altered the *ejido* system by which small farmers had enjoyed land security since the Mexican Revolution.

Violence is a form of consumerism that attempts to create a global marketplace, where homogenous consumers buy products promoted as "absolute necessities of the good life" by transnational companies. Cultural violence is the forceful replacement of indigenous culture with something imported.

Violence is also unemployment and underemployment, inhumane working conditions, and in some places, even slavery. Too often workers are pitted against each other across national boundaries and are vulnerable to the threats of canceled contracts or otherwise mobile capital in a world where borders are real for workers but nonexistent for capital.

For rural workers in many countries violence is also vastly unequal access to arable land and other essential natural resources. In Chile, for example, control of the best land and water resources has been systematically granted to large agribusiness companies, many of them foreign, specializing in fruit production and forestry. Family farms and cooperatives, the backbone of Chilean agriculture, are disappearing.

The United States is the most powerful member country of the World Bank, the International Monetary Fund (IMF), and other multilateral creditors to which poor countries are so heavily obligated. These and other international financial institutions like the World Trade Organization establish the rules of the global economy. Some of the decisions made by these institutions beyond the reach of most poor country governments include: a) how prices are set for basic commodities, so often the main export product for poor countries; b) what are "acceptable" levels of inflation for these countries; and c) how and when their markets should be opened to foreign products and investment.

New Directions

The U.S. government, U.S. banks and corporations, and U.S. consumers are also major players in the global marketplace, the freedom of which is staunchly supported by virtually every level of U.S. policy. In several arenas where the violent drama of the global economy is being played out, citizens of the United States have the opportunity to promote economic justice and an extremely important form of nonviolence.

Significant efforts are underway to ensure that multilateral, U.S. government, and U.S.private sector transnational actors are held accountable for the impact of their policies, programs, and projects on the human community and the rest of creation. In "Principles for Global Responsibility,"[5] the Interfaith Center on Corporate Responsibility (ICCR) wrote,

"Faith communities measure the global economy not only by what it produces, and its impact on the environment, but by how it touches human life and whether it protects or undermines the dignity of the human person. Economic decisions have human and moral consequences. Human dignity can only be realized and protected in solidarity with others. The protection of human rights — civil, political, social and economic — are minimum standards for social institutions that respect human dignity and social justice."

With the encouragement of religious institutions, labor organizations, development agencies, advocates for the rights of women and children, and many others, some companies are adopting codes of conduct for their international business activities. "Principles for Global Responsibility" proposes a new relationship between corporations and communities, underscores the importance of sustainable economic development, and stresses respect for the dignity of every human person and for collective and individual human rights.(26)

Consumers can play an important role in reducing economic violence. For example, a recent consumer campaign encouraged the popular GAP clothing stores to agree to enforce criteria for respecting workers' rights in Central American assembly plants working on GAP contracts.

Likewise, religious groups and many other nongovernmental organizations are exacting accountability from the international financial institutions. The World Bank and IMF are being challenged to respond to the lived experience of missioners and others who have lived among the poorest people in the world. Through efforts like *Rethinking Bretton Woods* of the Center of Concern and the *Religious Working Group on the World Bank and IMF* these powerful bodies are being called to reshape their procedures, their projects, and their policies.

Session 8

Nonviolent Social Change in Action: M.L. King, Jr. and the Civil Rights Movement

Session 8
Nonviolent Social Change in Action:
Martin Luther King, Jr.
and the Civil Rights Movement

Agenda

○ Opening meditation [1 min.]

○ Experiences or insights since the last session [10 min.]
○ Small groups [20 min.]
○ Large group [19 min.]

○ The journey of Martin Luther King, Jr. [5 min.]
○ Turning point [5 min.]
○ King's principles of nonviolence [35 min.]

○ Reflection on this section's reading [20 min.]
○ Conclusion [5 min.]

Supplemental Material

A. Case study: The 1963 Birmingham Campaign
B. The Stages of the Birmingham Campaign
C. Additional Recommended Reading
D. Session 8 Reading: "Fanny Lou Hamer: Baptsim by Fire," by Susan Kling

Session 8
Nonviolent Social Change in Action: Martin Luther King, Jr. and The Civil Rights Movement

Opening Meditation — 1 min.

We are now faced with the fact that tomorrow is today.
We are confronted with the fierce urgency of now.
In this unfolding conundrum of life and history
there is such a thing as being too late.
Procrastination is still the thief of time...
We must move past indecision to action...Now let us begin.
Now let us re-dedicate ourselves to the long and bitter —
and beautiful — struggle for a new world.
This is the calling of the children of God,
and our brothers and sisters wait eagerly for our response.
Shall we say the odds are too great?
Shall we tell them the struggle is too hard?
...Or will there be another message,
of longing, of hope, of solidarity with their yearnings,
of commitment to the cause, whatever the cost?
The choice is ours, and though we might prefer it otherwise
we must choose in this crucial moment in human history.

Martin Luther King, Jr.

Experiences or Insights Since the Last Session — 10 min.

Take a few minutes to reflect together on issues or experiences which this program has raised for the participants since the last gathering. Ask people if they would like to volunteer to share an excerpt from their nonviolence journals.

Small Groups — 15 min.

Members of the small groups are invited to reflect on the following (again, at whatever level that they feel comfortable):

O In what ways has Martin Luther King, Jr. and the Civil Rights movement impacted your life?

Large Group — 19 min.

O *Ask people to share an experience or insight that emerged during the small group reflection (again, at whatever level they feel comfortable).*

The Journey of Martin Luther King, Jr. — 5 min.

Ask people one by one to read aloud one section of the following overview of King's life and work:

O Martin Luther King trained for the ministry at Crozier Theological Seminary, and received his Ph.D in Theology from Boston University, where he was heavily influenced by the thought of Reinhold Neibuhr and Paul Tillich. (For a fascinating study of King's intellectual development, see John J. Ansbro, *Martin Luther King, Jr.: The Making of a Mind*, Maryknoll, NY: Orbis, 1982.) He planned to follow in the footsteps of his father, a successful, middle-class minister.

O King was appointed to the Dexter Avenue Baptist Church in Montgomery, Alabama in 1955. On December 1, Rosa Parks refused to move to the back of a Montgomery city bus, thus initiating a year-long bus boycott. The modern Civil Rights movement was born.

O The Montgomery Improvement Association — a group of church leaders spearheading the boycott — chose King as spokesperson: not because of his oratory and certainly not because of his virtually nonexistent experience, but because he was new in town and did not owe any allegiance to any existing faction.

O After Montgomery's African-American population boycotted the buses for twelve months, the city relented. The success of the campaign fueled similar actions across the U.S. and made King a visible and popular leader. During the bus boycott, King had been schooled in the principles of Gandhian nonviolence by long-time nonviolent strategist Bayard Rustin and Glenn Smiley. On staff with the Fellowship of Reconciliation, Smiley had been exploring ways nonviolent tactics could be applied to racism since first reading *War Without Violence*, written by Krishnalal Shridharani in 1939. This book was the first detailed analysis of Gandhi's nonviolent philosophy and tactics. At Smiley's urging, King traveled to India after the bus boycott to meet with Gandhi's successors.

O From 1955 until his assassination in 1968, King gave himself almost entirely to the movement for human dignity, which came to be known as the Civil Rights movement. Almost from the beginning, there were death threats and physical attacks,. He was arrested 200 times for acts. He was also the subject of ongoing government surveillance.

Turning Point — 5 min.

133

Read this section to the group:

During the Montgomery bus boycott, when things were going badly and when he had received a threat that his house would be bombed, King sat one night in his kitchen after midnight, feeling the weight of it all. Of this experience, Taylor Branch, in *Parting the Waters: America in the King Years, 1954-63* (New York: Simon & Schuster, 1988)

"King buried his face in his hands at the kitchen table. He admitted to himself that he was afraid, that he had nothing left, that the people would falter if they looked to him for strength. Then he said as much out loud. He spoke the name of no deity, but his doubts spilled out as a prayer, ending, "I've come to the point where I can't face it alone."

"As he spoke these words, the fears suddenly began to melt away. He became intensely aware of what he called an 'inner voice' telling him to do what he thought was right. Such simplicity worked miracles, bringing a shudder of relief and the courage to face anything.

"It was for King the first transcendent religious experience of his life."

○ After all the campaigns — in Montgomery, Selma, Birmingham, Chicago and many other places — King wistfully looked forward to the time when he could one day teach theology at a university and continue to pastor a church. Of course, this never happened. Those who met King toward the end of his life saw a kind of sadness, a sense that he was, as Rev. Phil Lawson put it, "abstaining from his preferences" because he was part of something much larger than himself, because "God takes you where you don't necessarily want to go." Nevertheless, there was peace in knowing that this was the place he was supposed to be.

"Boycotting buses in Montgomery, demonstrating in Birmingham, the citadel of segregation, and defying guns, dogs, and clubs in Selma, while maintaining disciplined nonviolence, totally confused the rulers of the South. If they let us march, they admitted their lie that the black man [sic] was content. If they shot us down, the told the world they were inhuman brutes. They tried to stop us by threats and fear, the tectic that had long worked so effectively. But nonvioence had muzzled their guns and Negro defiance had shaken their confidence. When they finally reached for clubs, dogs, and guns, they found the world was watching, and then the power of nonviolent protest became manifest."

M.L. King, Jr., *The Trumpet of Conscience*

King's Principles of Nonviolence — 30 min.

Have one person read one of these principles. Lead a large group discussion. Then have the next person read the next principle and repeat the process.

1) Nonviolence is a way of life for courageous people.

O It is active nonviolent resistance to evil.
O It is aggressive spiritually, mentally and emotionally.
O It is always persuading the opponent of the righteousness of your cause.

2) Nonviolence seeks to win friendship and understanding.

O The end result of nonviolence is redemption and reconciliation.
O The purpose of nonviolence is the creation of the Beloved Community.

3) Nonviolence seeks to defeat injustice, not people.

O Nonviolence holds that evil doers are also victims.
O The nonviolent resister seeks to defeat evil, not people.

4) Nonviolence holds that suffering can educate and transform.

O Nonviolence accepts suffering without retaliation.
O Nonviolence accepts violence if necessary, but will never inflict it.
O Nonviolence willingly accepts the consequences of its acts.
O Unearned suffering is redemptive and has tremendous educational and transforming possibilities.
O Suffering can have the power to convert the enemy when reason fails.

5) Nonviolence chooses love instead of hate.

O Nonviolence resists violence of the spirit as well as the body.
O Nonviolent love is spontaneous, unmotivated, unselfish and creative.
O Nonviolent love gives willingly, knowing that the return might be hostility.
O Nonviolent love is active, not passive.
O Nonviolent love is unending in its ability to forgive in order to restore community.
O Nonviolent love does not sink to the level of the hater.
O Love for the enemy is how we demonstrate love for ourselves.
O Love restores community and resists injustice.
O Nonviolence recognizes the fact that all life is interrelated.

6) Nonviolence believes that the universe is on the side of justice.

O The nonviolent resister has deep faith that justice will eventually win.
O Nonviolence believes that God is a God of justice and love.

Reflection on This Session's Reading:
"Fannie Lou Hamer: Baptism by Fire," by Susan Kling — 20 min.

Ask the participants to comment on what this article tells them about the nonviolence of the Civil Rights movement.

Conclusion — 5 min.

Nonviolence Journal

O *Offer a nonviolence journal topic for the next session:*
Please reflect on one of the six principles of nonviolence M.L. King, Jr. enunciated, both in terms of your personal life and in terms of transforming a contemporary social condition or policy.

Reading

O *Remind the participants to read all the material for the next session:*
1) The lesson plan for Session 9
2) The supplemental material for Session 9, and
3) The reading for Session 9: Servicio Paz y Justicia (SERPAJ)'s "Preparing for Nonviolence."

Evaluation

O *Hold a brief evaluation of this session:*
1. First, ask people to share the things that worked well, and
2. Ask them to share things that could be improved.

Closing Circle and Prayer

O *In a closing circle, share this statement from Martin Luther King, Jr.:*

"There is nothing wrong with a traffic law which says you have to stop for a red light. But when a fire is raging, the fire truck goes right through that red light.... Or when a [person] is bleeding to death, the ambulance goes through those red lights at top speed.... Disinherited people all over the world are bleeding to death from deep social and economic wounds. They need *brigades* of ambulance drivers who will have to ignore the red lights of their present system until the emergency is solved." (From Martin Luther King, Jr., *The Trumpet of Conscience* [New York: Harper & Row, 1967].)

Session 8: Supplemental Material

A. Case Study: The 1963 Birmingham Campaign

○ From 1955 through 1968, the Civil Rights Movement advanced its goals by launching a series of campaigns focused on a range of concrete injustices throughout the U.S. South and beyond. After the Montgomery bus boycott in 1955-56, the next key campaign was the effort to desegregate restaurants, which began in Greensboro, North Carolina in 1960. This was followed by the 1961 "freedom rides," in which African-Americans and non-African-Americans broke laws prohibiting integrated interstate travel. In 1962, the Albany movement (in the state of Georgia) set broad goals to end all segregation in that city. Even though this movement generated strong grassroots support, it was only partially successful. Movement strategists concluded that one of the key problems was that the goals had been too broad.

○ The Southern Christian Leadership Conference (SCLC), which King led, decided to be much more strategic in its next campaign. In January 1963 in Dorchester, Georgia, the SCLC held a strategy retreat in which it decided that the next desegregation campaign should focus on Birmingham because the injustice was very clear there and because the sheriff, Theophilus Eugene "Bull" Connor, had a reputation of documented abuse of African-Americans. They also decided that the goals would be narrow: desegregation of the city's downtown businesses. It was also decided that, if necessary, the movement would invite the children of Birmingham to join the campaign.

B. The Stages of the Birmingham Campaign

○ **January-March:** King prepares the ground with a speaking tour across the U.S.
○ **April 3:** The campaign begins with a mass meeting in a Birmingham church
○ **April 4:** 20 arrested picketing downtown store
○ **April 6:** 30 arrested at City Hall
○ **April 7:** Rev. A.D. King — Martin King's brother — leads a march, which is met by police wielding billy-clubs and German shepherds
○ **April 10:** A counter-move by the city: court injunction naming 133 civil rights leaders
○ **April 12 (Good Friday):** M.L. King breaks the injunction, leading 50 to jail. (Andrew Young has said of King's action, "That was, I think, the beginning of his true leadership.")

○ **April 12-20:** King kept in solitary confinement; he writes the "Letter from a Birmingham Jail"

○ Movement escalation: recruiting Birmingham's African-American schoolchildren as demonstrators

○ **May 2:** "Children's Crusade" begins; 959 arrested

○ **May 3:** 1,000 children participate in demonstration; some of the children are attacked by dogs and police wielding hoses; Birmingham's African-American community solidifies behind the campaign

○ Marches dramatically grow in size

○ **May 6:** 2,000 people in the city jail

○ **May 7:** During the demonstration, hoses and dogs are turned on people again. This is televised across the country, provoking nationwide outrage

○ The federal government intervenes and brokers a negotiated settlement

○ **May 10:** A settlement is announced — the city's lunch-counters are desegregated and the department stores agree to hire African-Americans in clerical and sales positions

○ The KKK riot and perpetrate bombings

○ New city government honors the settlement

○ The Birmingham Campaign spurs federal action on a new Civil Rights bill

○ The momentum of the Birmingham struggle leads to the organization of the historic August 1963 "March on Washington," during which 250,000 people demand passage of the bill.

C. Additional Recommended Reading

John J. Ansbro, *Martin Luther King, Jr.: The Making of a Mind* (Maryknoll, NY: Orbis Books, 1982).

Taylor Branch, *Parting the Waters: America in the King Years, 1954-63* (New York: Simon & Schuster, 1988).

Martin Luther King, Jr., "Letter from a Birmingham Jail," Why We Can't Wait (New York: A Signet Book, 1964).

_____"Nonviolence and Social Change," *Trumpet of Conscience* (New York: Harper and Row, 1967).

_____*Strength to Love* (New York: Harper & Row, 1963).

_____*Stride Toward Freedom* (New York: Harper & Brothers, 1958).

Juan Williams, *Eyes on the Prize: America's Civil Rights Years, 1954-1965* (New York: Viking, 1987).

Fannie Lou Hamer: Baptism by Fire

by Susan Kling

Then came the summer of '62, when the magic word "Freedom!" swept like a wild wind through the South. In late August, James Bevel of the Southern Christian Leadership Conference came down to Ruleville, Mississippi, and together with James Forman of the Student Nonviolent Coordinating Committee (SNCC) and other Black and white activists in the boiling civil rights movement, called a mass meeting at a church there.

Fannie Lou attended this gathering — and her life suddenly changed. "I had never heard the freedom songs before!" she said in wonder. And of the people she listened to: "They really wanted to change the world I knew — they wanted Blacks to register to vote!" They wanted Blacks to be able to have some small say about their destiny.

Fannie Lou felt that she was called, that this was the chance she had waited for, it seemed, all of her life. She and seventeen others in the church signed up to go to Sunflower County Courthouse the next Friday, to register to vote. Without any vote or special arrangement, Fannie Lou became the leader of the group. On the following Friday, August 31, she and the seventeen other Blacks, fearful but determined, boarded a bus owned by a friendly Black man, and rode to the courthouse in Indianola.

. Police and other whites began to mill around the bus when it stopped. But the eighteen, with Fannie Lou in front, marched bravely into the courthouse. There they were promptly told to go outside and come in two at a time.

Fannie Lou was asked twenty-one questions, including one that required her to copy and interpret a part of the constitution of Mississippi. "I could copy it, she said later, "but I sure couldn't interpret it — because up to that time, I hadn't even known Mississippi *had* a constitution." She failed the registration test, as did all the others. But she made up her mind that she would come back, no matter how many times, until she did pass.

In the late afternoon, after all the others with her had gone through the same frustrating, threatening day, with rifle-carrying whites strolling in and out of the courthouse past them, they boarded the bus and started for home. They had gone only a few miles when they were stopped by a policeman and ordered to return to Indianola. There the driver was fined $100 for driving a bus "with the wrong color."

The severe backlash against Fannie Lou began with that first effort to register to vote. But for her, that day was also the beginning of a new level of struggle against racism, which lasted for the rest of her life.

Here is the story of what happened when she tried to register, as taken from a hearing before the Select Panel on Mississippi and Civil Rights, held at the National Theater, Washington, D.C., on Monday, June 8,1964, and reprinted in the Congressional Record of June 16,1964:

"... I will begin from the first beginning, August 31, in 1962. I traveled twenty-six miles to the county courthouse to try to register to become a first class citizen. I was fired the 31st of August in 1962 from a plantation where I had worked as a timekeeper and a sharecropper for eighteen years. My husband had worked there thirty years.

"I was met by my children when I returned from the courthouse, and my girl (her eldest daughter) and my husband's cousin told me that this man my husband worked for was raising a lot of Cain. I went on in the house, and it wasn't long before my husband came and said this plantation owner said I would have to leave if I didn't go down and withdraw.

"...(The plantation owner) said, 'Fannie Lou, you have been to the courthouse to try and register,' and he said, 'We are not ready for this in Mississippi.' I said, 'I didn't register for you, I tried to register for myself.' He said, 'We are not going to have this in Mississippi, and you will have to withdraw. I am looking for your answer yea or nay.'

"I just looked. He said, 'I will give you until tomorrow morning.'

"So I just left the same night."

She told the panel her husband was not allowed to leave the plantation until after harvest time, but in spite of this restriction, he took his wife to the home of a friend in Ruleville. She also said that the plantation owner had warned her husband, Pap, that if he decided to go with Fannie Lou their furniture would be confiscated and Pap would lose his job. Thus, because of the need for the family to have housing and some means of her husband earning a livelihood, Fannie Lou was forced to separate from her husband.

Her report to the panel continued, "On the 10th of September, they fired into the home of Mr. and Mrs. Robert Cuker sixteen times, for me. That same night, two girls were shot at Mr. Herman Sissel's; also, they shot into Mr. Joe Maglon's house. I was fired at that day, and haven't had a job since ...."

Her husband was fired anyway and the furniture confiscated by the plantation owner, who took their car as well, saying they owed him $300 on it.

Fannie Lou became a virtual fugitive, staying here and there with friends or distant relatives. At last the family found a bare house into which they moved. But even here, they were not left in peace. Cars full of white men armed with rifles would ride up and back in front of the house, shouting obscenities and threatening to shoot.

If any of the family left the house, for whatever reason, cars followed, with white men leaning out of the windows, shouting, cursing and threatening. But these reprisals, as well as the abusive letters that she kept receiving, only stiffened her resolve and made her more determined to keep to the path on which she had set her feet. And her family, to their everlasting credit, stood solidly with her.

At last, word of what was happening to her reached the ears of the

Student Nonviolent Coordinating Committee. Robert Moses, a leader in the Mississippi grassroots civil rights movement, came down to Ruleville and invited Fannie Lou to attend a SNCC conference at Fisk University in Nashville, Tennessee, in the fall of 1962. That conference instilled in her an even more total commitment, and she went to work for SNCC, "even when they didn't have any money." This work provided her with a kind of security, for after that she never felt alone in the ideals she had laid out for herself.

She not only worked for SNCC as a Field Secretary, but was tireless in half a dozen other avenues as well. She circulated a petition to get food and clothing from the government for needy families. She helped in getting welfare programs started, she got clothes from people who didn't need them to people who did, and she cooked for the many volunteer workers who continually came to help. In addition to all of this work, she was employed for a time at a Ruleville cotton gin, until she was fired for attempting to register Blacks to vote. She had to leave her house again.

When she returned to the Sunflower County Courthouse on December 4th to take the registration test a second time, as she explained later, "There was nothing they could do to me. They couldn't fire me, because I didn't have a job. They couldn't put me out of my house, because I didn't have one. There was nothing they could take from me any longer." She told them, "You'll see me every thirty days, until I pass." And on January 10, 1963, she passed and became one of the first of Sunflower County's 30,000 Blacks to register to vote.

But on June 3, 1963, she paid heavily for that right and for the work she was doing to get Blacks to register.

"I had gone to a voter education workshop in Charleston, South Carolina," she told the Congressional Panel. "We left Mississippi June 3, 1963. We finished the workshop June 8th. We left on the 8th by Continental Trailways bus, returning back to Mississippi.

"We arrived in Winona, Mississippi, between 10:30 and 11 a.m., June 9th. Four of our group got off the bus to get food in the bus terminal. Two got off to use the washroom. I was still on the bus. I saw six people rush out, and I got off to see what was happening.

"Miss Ann Ponder told me the chief of police and a state highway patrolman had ordered them out. I said, 'Well this is Mississippi for you.' I went and got back on the bus.

"I looked out of the window and they were putting the Negroes in a car. I was holding Miss Ponder's iron. I got off to ask her what to do with it. My friends shouted, 'Get back on the bus!'

"A white officer said to me, 'You are under arrest. Get in the car.' As I went to get in, he kicked me. In the car, they would ask me questions. When I started to answer, they would curse and tell me to hush, and call me awful names.

"They carried me to the (Montgomery) County jail. Later I heard Miss Ponder's voice and the sound of kicks. She was screaming awfully.

"Then three white men came to my room. A state highway policeman (he had the marking on his sleeve) asked me where I was from. I said, 'Ruleville.' He said, 'We're goin' to check that.' They left out. They came back and he said, 'You're damn rightl!'

"They said they were going to make me wish I was dead. They had me lay down on my face, and they ordered two Negro prisoners to beat me with a blackjack. That was unbearable. It was leather, loaded with something.

"The first prisoner beat me until he was exhausted. Then the second Negro began to beat. I have a limp. I had polio when I was about six years old. I was holding my hands behind me to protect my weak side. I began to work (move) my feet. The state highway patrolman ordered the other Negro to sit on my feet.

"My dress pulled up and I tried to smooth it down. One of the policemen walked over and raised my dress as high as he could. They beat me until my body was hard, 'til I couldn't bend my fingers or get up when they told me to. That's how I got this blood clot in my left eye — the sight's nearly gone, now. And my kidney was injured from the blows they gave me in the back."

She was left in the cell, bleeding and battered, listening to the screams of Ann Ponder, who was being beaten in another cell, and hearing the white men talk of "plotting to kill us, maybe to throw our bodies in the Big Black River, where nobody would ever find us."

At last, word of the beatings and detention at Winona reached the ears of Dr. Martin Luther King, Jr., who sent members of his staff to the jail, with the demand that Fannie Lou and the others be released at once. Andrew Young and James Bevel came to the jail, helped carry her out, half conscious, and took her to a doctor in Greenwood, Mississippi, where the blood was washed off her,and her wounds stitched and bandaged. Then they took her to Atlanta to some friends of the civil rights movement, where she remained for a month, convalescing. During this month, she refused to allow her husband to come to see how terrible she looked, until some of the scars were less livid and the swelling had gone down. While she had been in the Winona jail, she told friends, "Medger Evers was killed, and they offered to let us go one night, but I knew it was just so they could kill us, and say we was trying to escape. I told 'em they'd have to kill me in my cell." (George Sewell, *The Black Collegian*, May/June, 1978).

The effects of the beatings plagued Fannie Lou for the rest of her life, until sometimes she would say caustically, "I'm sick and tired of being sick and tired!"

This brutal experience only served to make her more determined than ever to continue to get Blacks to register. As soon as she was able, even limping and almost nauseated with pain, she was out in the cotton fields at sun up, lining up prospective voters, and telling them how almighty powerful it would be to be able to vote. Evenings she spent going around to the many little churches in the countryside, talking about voter registration, and singing in that powerful voice that moved all who heard her sing the freedom songs she had learned. But her base was always Ruleville, where she had been born and raised.

Neither the beating nor the constant hate letters and abusive telephone calls she received deterred her from her work, and she refused to move away. "I ain't goin' no place," she insisted. "I have a right to stay here. With all that my parents and grandparents gave to Mississippi, I have a right to stay here and fight for what they didn't get." And after her experience in the Winona jail, she added, "I don't want equal rights no more. I don't want to be equal to men that beat us. I want human rights!" (Phyl Garland, "Builders of a New South," *Ebony Magazine*, August 1966).

Session 9

Experimenting with Nonviolence: Creating Nonviolent Activity

Session 9
Experimenting with Nonviolence:
Creating Nonviolent Activity

Agenda

○ Opening meditation [1 min.]

○ Experiences or insights since the last session [10 min.]
○ Small groups [15 min.]
○ Large group [15 min.]

○ The consensus process [10 min.]
○ Consensus role-play [10 min.]

Reflection on this section's reading [15 min.]

○ Creating a nonviolent action [15 min.]
○ Becoming clear about the goal of the activity [10 min.]
○ Constructing the nonviolent activity [14 min.]

○ Conclusion [5 min.]

Supplemental Material

A. Additional recommended reading
B. Session 9 Reading: "Preparing for Nonviolence," by Servicio Paz y Justicia

Session 9
Experimenting with Nonviolence:
Creating Nonviolent Activity

Opening Meditation: The United Farm Workers Prayer
— 1 min.

Show me the suffering of the most miserable;
     so I will know my people's plight.
Free me to pray for others;
     for You are present in every person.
Help me take responsibility for my own life;
     so that I can be free at last.
Grant me courage to serve others;
     for in service there is true life.
Give me honesty and patience;
     so that the Spirit will be alive among us.
Let the Spirit flourish and grow;
     so that we will never tire of the struggle.
Let us remember those who have died for justice;
     for they have given us life.
Help us love even those who hate us;
     so we can change the world. Amen.

Cesar Chavez

Experiences or Insights Since the Last Session — 10 min.

Take a few minutes to reflect together on issues or experiences which this program has raised for the participants since the last gathering. Ask people if they would like to volunteer to share an excerpt from their nonviolence journals.

Small Groups — 15 min.

Members of the small groups are invited to reflect on the following (again, at whatever level each feels comfortable):

○ What are some of the public forms of violence and injustice that you would like to transform through nonviolence?

Large Group — 10 min.

○ *Ask people to reassemble and to share an experience or insight that emerged during the small group reflection (again, at whatever level they feel comfortable).*

The Consensus Process — 10 min.

As a way of experimenting with the ideas and tools the group has been exploring in this program, invite the group to participate in creating and carrying out a group nonviolent activity.

Share this material:

To create a group activity, we need a decision-making process. The consensus process is a method of group decision-making by which an entire group of people can come to an agreement. The input and ideas of all participants are gathered and synthesized to arrive at a final decision acceptable to all. Through consensus, we are not only working to achieve better solutions, but also to promote the growth of community and trust. It is also a process which invests everyone in the outcome, and in the responsibility to carry it out. (*This material is drawn from Butigan, Messman and Pastrick, eds.,* Basta! No Mandate for War *[Philadelphia: New Society Publishers, 1984], pp. 49-50.)*

○ Consensus vs. Voting: Voting is a means by which we choose one alternative from several. Consensus, on the other hand, is a process of synthesizing many diverse elements together. Voting is a win or lose model in which people are more concerned with the numbers it takes to win than with the issue itself. Voting does not take into account individual feelings or needs. In essence it is a quantitative, rather than qualitative, method of decision-making.

○ With consensus, people can and should work through differences together and synthesize seemingly contradictory ideas. We believe that people are able to talk peacefully about their differences and reach a mutually satisfactory position. It is possible for one person's insights or strongly held beliefs to sway the whole group. No ideas are lost; each member's input is valued as part of the solution.

○ Consensus does not mean everyone thinks the decision made is necessarily the best one possible, or even that they are sure it will work. What it does mean is that in coming to this decision, no one feels her or his position is misunderstood or that it isn't given a fair hearing. It also means that the final decision doesn't violate someone's fundamental moral values, for if it did they would be obligated to block consensus. It is hoped that everyone will think it's the best decision; this often happens because, when it works, collective intelligence does come up with better solutions than could individuals. But occasionally it may not. Those who object can do one of several things:

○ Give qualified support ("I don't see the need for this, but I'll go along with it.")
○ Stand aside ("I think it's a mistake but I can live with it.")
○ Block ("I cannot support this or allow the group to support it. It is immoral.")
○ Withdraw from the group.

If someone blocks, they are encouraged to present a new proposal.

○ The steps of the consensus process include:

○ Someone puts forward a proposal
○ The facilitator asks if there are any qualifying questions
○ Then the facilitator asks if there are any reservations
○ If there are strong reservations, the facilitator asks for any amendments
○ After the proposal is amended, the facilitator asks for consensus
○ If no one blocks, then consensus is reached
○ Often it is helpful to restate the proposal so everyone is clear on its content.

Consensus Role-Play — 10 min.

Ask the participants to break into small groups and use the consensus process to role-play ordering a pizza.

Reflection on This Session's Reading:
"Preparing for Nonviolence" by Servicio Paz y Justicia
— 10 min.

Highlight the key points. Ask people to discuss what struck them about the process of creating a nonviolent activity.

Creating A Nonviolent Action — 15 min.

Normally, a group seeking to create a nonviolent activity has come together with a specific focus: ending harassment of homeless people, or stopping racist acts, or contributing to a nuclear-free future. In this program, people have a wide variety of interests. In this part of Session Nine, ask the participants to brainstorm on what they would like to focus.

As a first step, the participants are invited to sit in a circle and get into a relaxed position. Let the room grow quiet. Allow your deepest self to speak. What is it, in your core, you want to see addressed? It can be something close at hand — the need for a stop sign at a busy street corner — or it can be international in scope. It could be declaring "Nonviolence Day" for one day, with your group standing in a busy part of town handing out leaflets with Martin Luther King's six principles of nonviolence. It could be participating in something already planned.

Ask participants to share their thoughts on an issue they would like to address. See if the group can reach consensus on its focus. After that process, let's try to get more specific: what kind of an activity would they like to construct — and what would be its goal?

Becoming Clear About the Goal of the Activity — 10 min.

Role-play the issue. Form a circle with four-six pieces of paper on the floor. Write the names of the different parties of the conflict. Have people stand on the piece of paper and role-play that particular point of view. After 2 minutes, each person rotate to the next piece of paper to the right, and assumes that new position. Do this until you have gone all around the circle. This will help think through the various views of this issue, but also of the action you want to create. For example, if you wanted to address police harassment of homeless people, the positions might include homeless women and men themselves, police officers, the mayor, the press, members of neighborhood groups, people with business interests, and general tax-payers.

Constructing the Nonviolent Activity — 14 min.

Facilitate the process by which an action is created. The following issues should be considered:

○ What are the specific objectives of the event?
○ How will you communicate your objectives to your audience before, during, and after the event?
○ Will you be trying to make allies with other groups or communities?
○ Do you need sub-committees to plan various aspects of the activity?
○ What will the scenario be?
○ Will you need props and other materials?
○ Will you have a flyer, explaining to the public what you are doing?
○ What publicity will you do? Will you try to reach other people to join you?

- What kind of media work will you do? Will you send out a press release ahead of time? Will there be spokespeople during the event, ready to talk to the press? Will they have a series of "talking points"?
- Will you need to raise money for the event? How will you do this?
- What about the logistics of the event? Will you need a stage? A sound system? A truck to transport materials? Car-pooling?
- Will you need peace-keepers or monitors to ensure that the event remains nonviolent?
- Who will clean up after the event?

Once you have decided on your activity — and settled on a date and place — you should break into small sub-committees to handle the various tasks associated with the event.

Once the groups have done their work, all should report back in the large group so that everyone can see how it all fits together.

Conclusion — 5 min.

Nonviolence Journal

- *Offer a nonviolence journal topic for the next session:*
  What other social justice issues do you want to address?

Reading

- *Remind the participants of to read all the material for the next session:*
1) The lesson plan for Session 10
2) The supplemental material for Session 10, and
3) The reading for Session 10: Bill Cane's "The Church Universal: Circles of Faith."

Evaluation

- *Hold a brief evaluation of this session:*
1. First, ask people to share the things that worked well, and
2. Ask them to share things that could be improved.

Closing Circle and Prayer

- *Closing circle: A brief comment on the implications for nonviolence of the philosopher Schaupenhauer's statement:*

Truth passes through three phases.
> First, it is ridiculed.
> Second, it is violently opposed.
> Third, it becomes self-evident.

Session 9: Supplemental Material

Additional Recommended Reading

Angie O'Gorman, "Defense Through Disarmament: Nonviolence
and Personal Assault," Angie O'Gorman, ed., *The Universe Bends
Toward Justice: A Reader on Christian Nonviolence*
(Philadelphia: New Society Publishers, 1990), pp. 241-247.

Session 9 Reading:

Preparing for Nonviolence

by Servicio Paz y Justicia

The following document from the Brazilian branch of the international Servicio Paz y Justicia (SERPAJ) nonviolence network explores the principles of firmeza permanente *[literally "relentless persistence"] from the perspective of the popular movements there and discusses the need for and the content of training for nonviolent action. It reflects the time (the mid-1970s) and the setting (Brazil) in which it is written. Nevertheless, it offers us critical insights which can be used to guide our contemporary efforts to organize nonviolent activity in a wide variety of contexts.*

Convictions and Consequences of Active Nonviolence

Active nonviolence offers to both the oppressed and the oppressor the possibility of safeguarding their honor and their person. In the unjust, it attempts to nurture understanding, transformation, and even collaboration toward the good of all. It does not seek the humiliation of the enemy, nor his or her destruction, and it is careful not to be unnecessarily provocative.

This struggle enriches the adversaries—both aggressor and victim. Even if in the first stage of the struggle the victims are not able to achieve their objectives or to emerge victorious, they should not allow apparent failure to discourage them or diminish their struggle. Even without immediate positive or visible results, our conviction—and the guarantee of nonviolent action—is that truth and loving action have within them an all-encompassing, redeeming, and life-giving value: "To wish to save all humankind, including the oppressor."

This "universality" of the act of liberating nonviolence has infinite repercussions in the lives of men and women. Active nonviolence seeks to be the expression of authentic love at the core of political combat.

Some Principles of Nonviolence

1. In order to attain a just society, we need means that are better than intrigue, plotting, *coups d'état*, torture, murder, and terrorism. To achieve justice and peace it is necessary to find just and peaceful means. Since such means are consistent with the ends we desire in the long run, they will be simpler and more effective.

2. *Firmeza permanente* or "relentless persistence," a term sometimes used in place of active nonviolence, is in no way cowardly submission to the oppressors. On the contrary, it opposes the tyrants and the violent ones with all its strength. The *practitioner of nonviolence* continually attempts to overcome bad with good, lies with truth, hatred with love.

3. The struggle of *firmeza permanente* draws all of its strength from truth. To withdraw from truth is to withdraw from the source of our strength. Therefore the struggle cannot be clandestine. If you act in secret, you end up lying in order to disguise your efforts.

4. Violence may be impressive at first sight if it is part of a courageous search for justice. With time, however, we find that the way of violence does not deliver the hoped for result.

5 . Courage in isolation is not enough. The struggle must be collective and organized. The struggle brings persecutions, but persecution and the action of the group nurture a class consciousness.

6. If the people do not want to use the very weapons that dehumanize the oppressor, the only solution is to accept, without retreating, the blows and the brutality of the adversary. There is no such thing as a human being who wishes to be inhuman until the end. Such is our hope.

7. Those who use violence attempt to provoke the practitioner of non-violence in order to get them to abandon their principal weapon: the use of *firmeza permanente*.

8. In a situation of weakness, *firmeza permanente* is more effective than violence.

9. By overcoming the oppressor through violence, one achieves only a partial victory. The roots of injustice remain within the oppressor who was defeated and within the victor who is liberated from the oppressor, since both used violence and so kept within themselves the evil that they fought.

10. We cannot offer any guarantees to anybody that they will not be imprisoned. We can only guarantee that we will go together and nobody will skip out on the others.

11. Since its first commitment is to truth and justice, *firmeza permanente* is not limited to strictly legal actions.

12. Violence comes from aggressive impulses that are not channeled constructively. Since it is irrational it leads to hatred. The practitioner of nonviolence, fed by the conviction that we are all brothers and sisters, aspires to act for justice through the control of reason over instinct.

13. Violence is often impatient. *Firmeza permanente* endeavors to wait and to respect the necessary stages, recognizing that the conservatives know how to compromise or to change when they need to.

14. In the face of the practitioner of nonviolence, the anger and the might of the oppressor are useless. He loses his sense of self-assurance because of the attitude of the victim and the appeals to reason that the victim makes. The transformation and the defeat that he suffers then are moral. Instead of humiliating him, they enrich him.

15. The important thing is not to be brave once in a while, but rather persistent all of the time. "We may die, but we are not going to run," pledged the workers of PERUS in the strike of 1967.

16. If you cannot commit yourself to be nonviolent, be violent. What you cannot be is submissive.

17. When somebody attacks another in an act of physical violence and the victim replies in kind or flees, the response of the victim gives the aggressor a great security and moral support, since it shows that the moral values of the victim are the same as those of the attacker. Any attitude of fight or flight on the part of the victim reinforces the morale of the aggressor. But if the attitude of the victim is calm and firm, the fruit of self-discipline and self-control, the aggressor is disarmed by the show of love and the respect for him or her as a person. This only happens because the victim does not respond to the violence of the aggressor either with cowardice or with counter-violence. Instead the victim attacks the aggressor at the level of thought, of intelligence, of reason, using the weapons of truth, justice, and love.

Training for Nonviolent Action

Firmeza permanente is not improvised. We must take training for nonviolent action seriously. *Firmeza permanente* requires training that is as much spiritual as practical, as much in the inspiration as in the tactics of nonviolence.

Analysis and Method

We do not propose to elaborate an overall strategy to resolve [for example] the land tenure problem nor to offer complete solutions... This is necessary, but we must be more modest. What we want to do is simply to offer some ideas that perhaps will help us to resist and attack in the way of active nonviolence when violent conflicts like these emerge. Let us consider a specific example.

In a factory, three workers file a complaint against the company. In accordance with the law, they are seeking salaries equal to those of other workers who are doing the same work. After various unsuccessful attempts to reach an agreement, they ask for a meeting with the manager. How should they prepare for this conversation/conflict, knowing that the company has a number of lawyers backing it, while they only have the assistance of the one union lawyer who has to handle many other cases besides? One method of preparation is to play out a "socio-drama."

Socio-Drama

Socio-drama is one of the best known and undoubtedly one of the most emotionally engaging training methods. It is a preview, in the form of theater, of a conflict that the participants are actually going to encounter. For example:

The case of the workers: Role play the conversation between the workers and the manager. Each one should give careful attention to preparing his or her role. Who will play the part of the manager and how? Of the workers? Of the lawyer from the union who accompanies them? Of the boss's secretary? Imagine the content of the conversation, the ambiance, the arguments each side will use. Anticipate the emotional reactions of the manager, the feelings of the workers. Divide up the tasks: During the conversation, who is going to speak? When? What tactic will you use?

The organizer who will train the others in this socio-drama should define with great care the theme (the principal problem which will be confronted), the setting (what will the environment be like?) and the place (where?) of the action. The roles of the other persons who are present should also be explained in detail. The actors assume their roles while the other members of the group constitute the public. Each person takes a few moments to get into his or her role and then the simulation begins. When the coordinator gives a signal, the simulation is stopped and the group critiques the actors. Did they represent, or better said, really express the feelings of the boss? Of the workers? Of the union representative? Was it realistic? Were there mistakes? Insights? Would the tactic they used work? Did the arguments carry weight? Are there other approaches?

Evaluation of the Socio-Drama

The goal of *firmeza permanente* is the efficacy of nonviolence. We want to achieve the objective without anyone dying, either morally or physically. A socio-drama permits us to evaluate realistically the resources that we actually have to carry an action through to the end.... Among the innumerable advantages that the socio-drama offers, we would single out the following:

1) It situates the action in its actual setting: the place (where will it be?); the time (exactly when? For how long?).

2) It familiarizes the participants with the situations in which they are engaged. Through the physical and emotional reactions that surface in the training, they are able to develop more appropriate responses to various situations, such as contact with the adversary, prison, shooting, negotiations with the authorities, surprise developments. This practical preparation for nonviolent action is very important because the diverse exercises enable one to take into account the psychological factors (critical to the course of an action), the rational factors (cool analysis of what should in fact be done), and the practical factors (which a simple theoretical study of the situation would not allow one to foresee). As such, the goal of a socio-drama goes far beyond traditional, superficial preparation, sitting around a table.

3) It attempts to comprehend the position of the adversary. This is an important step in nonviolence. It is necessary to put oneself in the place of the adversary in order to know why s/he acts in that manner. In this way, it is possible to prevent irresponsible actions in which the only result is to uselessly provoke the adversary and reinforce his or her error. There is no point in humiliating one's opponent. Rather, through truth and justice, we must find an honorable way out for everyone. Experiencing the difficulties that the adversary must overcome enables us to discover the adversary's strong points and, as a result, makes our action more effective, because we will know when and where to act to maximize the chances of success.

4) It reinforces and nurtures the unity of the group. How? It develops the confidence of each individual in the group, stretches the bonds of friendship, and familiarizes the group with tense situations. Often the training enables the discharge of internal tensions, allowing each individual to regain a sense of calm at the time of the action.

5) It reinforces and nurtures self-confidence in each individual. This is a crucial aspect. This trust in oneself develops if the person comprehends that she or he has the power to react in certain situations, that she or he is a member of a group that offers support, and finally, that she or he can take part in the unfolding of a situation in which the phases are known and understood. She or he is no longer a pawn.

6) It teaches the group to do self-evaluation. Evaluation is the essential phase of the training. It gives an opportunity to judge the success or failure of the exercise and, above all, to see whether or not adequate resources actually exist to undertake an action. New and original ideas come up to overcome obstacles. There is no training without evaluation...

Spiritual Training

Finally, we cannot forget this fundamental aspect of training. The apostle Paul reminds us that even in the most dramatic situations, "The fruit of the Spirit is love, joy, peace, patience, kindness, goodness, trustfulness, gentleness, and self-control." (Galatians 5:22).

Fasting and prayer are powerful weapons of nonviolence. Before any action that is likely to awaken the strongest passions, everyone should do such things as increase their vigils of prayer, ask the pardon of their brothers and sisters, purify themselves of evil, do justice in their own life, and fast.

Why all of this? Because we believe in the power of truth. It is truth that is going to triumph in the social, political, and other realms of human endeavor. Gandhi wrote: "By its very nature, truth gives evidence of itself. From the moment we leave behind all the stubborn webs of ignorance, the truth shines in splendor.... The way of truth is full of unimaginable obstacles. But in the faithful lover of truth there is neither deception nor defeat. For the truth is all-powerful, and the disciple of truth can never be overcome."

Translated from the Portuguese by
Philip McManus

Session 10

Creating
Communities
of
Nonviolence

Session 10
Creating Communities of Nonviolence

Agenda

○ An opening meditation [1 min.]

○ Experiences or insights since the last session [10 min.]

○ Evaluation of the group nonviolent activity [15 min.]

○ Milling exercise [5 min.]
○ Small groups [15 min.]
○ Large group [10 min.]

○ Reflecting on this section's reading [15 min.]

○ Nonviolence and community [15 min.]

○ What are our next steps? [15 min.]

○ Evaluation [10 min.]

○ Conclusion and commissioning [9 min.]

Supplemental Materials

A. Additional reading for this session
B. Session 10 Reading: "The Church Universal: Circles of Faith,"
   by Bill Cane

Session 10

Creating Communities of Nonviolence

An Opening Meditation: "A Case for Utopia" -- 1 min.

The world would be better off
if people tried to become better,
and people would be better
if they stopped trying to become better off.
For when everyone tries to become better off,
nobody is better off.
But when everyone tries to become better
everyone is better off.
Everyone would be rich
if nobody tried to become richer,
and nobody would be poor
if everyone tried to be the poorest.
And everybody would be what [she] ought to be
if everybody tried to be what [she] wants the other fellow to be.
Peter Maurin, co-founder with Dorothy Day
of the Catholic Worker movement

Experiences or Insights Since the Last Session — 10 min.

Take a few minutes to reflect together on issues or experiences which this program has raised for the participants since the last gathering. Ask if anyone would like to volunteer to share an excerpt from their nonviolence journals.

Evaluation of the Group Nonviolent Activity — 15 min.

Ask participants to:

○ List the positive dimensions of the action.
○ List the things that could be improved next time.
○ What did you learn through this process?

Milling Exercise — 5 min.

For process, see Section 1. Comments after each of the two times people "mill":

○ This person before you quite likely has a longing for nonviolence not only in their lives, but in their world. *(After a moment of silence:)* Let us acknowledge this truth in some way.

○ How are we to take the insights and practice of active nonviolence with us into the world? We can only do this well by being supported by a community moving toward the goal of becoming fully human. The person you are with is part of this community. *(After a moment of silence:)* Let us acknowledge this truth in some way or another.

After this exercise is over, invite each pair to join with another pair to form a four-person group.

Small Groups — 15 min.

Members of the small groups are invited to reflect on the following (again, at whatever level each feels comfortable):

○ What experiences have you had that might give you a glimpse of a "nonviolent culture" or a "nonviolent community"?

○ What would this look like? What steps do you think we — those of us in this room — need to take in order to build a "culture of nonviolence"?

Large Group — 10 min.

○ *Then, ask people to share an experience or insight that emerged during the small group reflection (again, at whatever level they feel comfortable).*

Reflecting on This Session's Reading:
The Church Universal: Circles of Faith" by Bill Cane — 15 min.

Ask people to discuss these questions:
○ How can we apply some of Bill Cane's ideas?

○ Why are communities of nonviolence important?

Nonviolence and Community — 15 min.

Ask one person to read one of the points below, then have the next read one, and so on.

○ Nonviolence nourishes, mends and celebrates the relationships that make our lives possible. Its vision is one of connectedness, not of rugged individualism. Ultimately, nonviolence seeks to create healthy and flourishing communities.

○ The heart of nonviolence is the process of building communities of care and respect. For emotional, spiritual and logistical reasons, it is the nonviolence community — perhaps a handful of people — which creates the support system for this work. For the truth is that the spiritual journey of nonviolence is extremely difficult if we undertake it by ourselves. In many ways, such individualism contradicts the heart of nonviolence. Nonviolence communities give us a place to reflect, to grapple with dilemmas, to mourn, to debrief.

○ The original vision of church was of a place to support the difficult work of proclaiming and living out the Gospel of love and justice. We need to reclaim this vision, bringing it alive in our institutions and our small groups. Church can again become one of the key sites where we name and nurture the "ministry of nonviolence" to which we are all called.

○ Such communities offer the opportunity to share and reflect on our lives, as well as to create practical visions in tackling the violence and injustice in our lives and in the life of the world.

○ These communities will become increasingly important as we struggle to create alternatives in a world where violence is pervasive. It is out of these communities that we will be able to effectively carry out a ministry of nonviolence.

What Are Our Next Steps? — 15 min.

Lead a session in deciding on the next concrete action of this group.

Evaluation -- 10 min.

Ask participants to evaluate the entire ten session course. First, ask people to list the things that worked well for them; second, ask them to share things that could be improved. Please take notes and, if you are willing, please share them with us at Pace e Bene so that we can learn what the strengths and weaknesses of this program are.

Conclusion and Commissioning — 9 min.

○ *Hold an evaluation of this session and the entire program: first what worked well, and second, things that could be improved.*

○ *Commissioning. Light a candle in the center of the room. Call the participants into the circle and commission them in this ministry of nonviolence. Use the prayer below or create one yourself.*

Spirit of God,
you hold us in Your embrace.
Your presence burns through this world,
transforming it.
You hold us in Your embrace.
You call us to see confront the mystery of evil.
You hold us in Your embrace.
You call us to live the astonishing mystery of good in the face
of the mystery of evil.
You hold us in Your embrace.
Be with us as we experiment with your nonviolence.
You hold us in Your embrace.
Give us the strength to break the rules of war,
to move from the war zone to the house of love.
You hold us in Your embrace.
We are grateful for You and for each other.

You hold us in Your embrace.
You hold us in Your embrace.
You hold us in Your embrace.

Session 10: Supplemental Material

A. Additional Recommended Reading For This Session

Shelley Douglass, "Taking Care," *Ground Zero* (Winter 1992), p. 1. Available from Ground Zero Center for Nonviolent Action, 16159 Clear Creek Road NW, Poulsbo, WA 98370.

William D. Miller, "Introduction," *A Harsh and Dreadful Love: Dorothy Day and the Catholic Worker Movement* (New York: Liveright, 1973), pp. 5-16.

The Church Universal: Circles of Faith

by Bill Cane

The call to live a spirited life is not a call to self-satisfaction or self-complacency, but to self-transcendence. We are constantly being called out of our present existence, to form circles that do not yet exist.

Some years ago, I had a dream. I was standing alone in a small clearing amid trees and crags and gray boulders when I suddenly saw a large opening in the rocky hillside facing me. The wall of the opening was made of clear glass, as were the doors. Through the glass I could see a cavernous room with a number of people standing around talking excitedly to each other. Above the entrance, in red letters that could have been from San Francisco's Chinatown, hung a sign which said: "THE CHURCH OF THE TAI CHI."

A woman inside was beckoning to me through the glass doors. I did not recognize her, and looked around to see if perhaps she was waving to someone else, but no one else was there. I pointed to myself and motioned, "Me?" She nodded reassuringly, and again invited me in with a wave of her hand. I entered the group and felt immediately at home. At the time, I did not know the meaning of the words "tai chi," and I had no idea what the dream meant. I even took a course in tai chi movement at a local college to see if the course would enlighten me, but it did not.

Years later, I realized that the dream had been introducing me to a different sort of "church." Tai chi literally means "universal wholeness." I was being invited to become part of a more universal and less structured church—part of a gathering of people who were serving "universal wholeness." They were not known to me and they did not hold regular weekly meetings. They were "hidden" and gathered at a depth "beneath the surface," but the entrance to their meeting place was open and they were easily recognized and joined once one had "located" oneself near them.

The original meaning of the word "church" (*ekklesia* for the Christians and *kahal* for the Jews) was neither a building for worship nor a weekly gathering. It was a coming together of people who were being called out of slavery to a new life of freedom. They were asked to believe in a dream, in a story that had not yet happened and seemed at the time to have not even the slightest chance of becoming history! They dedicated their lives to making this new story happen, and this was their faith.

The words *kahal* and *ekklesia*, synagogue and church, originally meant people called out—people called to leave the ordinary existence around them and enter a new life. Following Moses or Jesus was no ordinary life. It meant leaving security behind and becoming part of shaky and radical movements. But these movements promised an abundance of spirit and life in the future.

The existence people were called to enter did not yet exist. When the Jews defied the power of Pharaoh and left their homes, they spent forty years wandering in the desert. They did not know where they were going and had only the food they could gather for the day. When the early Christians dared to call Jesus Lord (*Xristos Kurios*) in a world where only Caesar could be called Lord (*Kurios Kaesar*), they were seen as subverting the established political order. For this, many of them faced persecution and death. They remained a struggling group at the margins of society for a century or more. If we look at present-day Christianity or Judaism in our country, we can find in them very little resemblance to their radical roots. Most adherents are comfortable within the established order, within an existence that already exists.

For [historian] Eugene Rosenstock-Huessy, entering a new existence that did not yet exist meant turning his back on the prevailing institutions of his society. As a young soldier returning to Germany from World War I, he was offered a position in the government, a job as head of a major religious publishing house, and a chair at the university. He agonized over the decision he had to make and then, unexpectedly, he turned down all three offers! It was years before Hitler would come to power, yet Rosenstock already recognized the smell of death in the society. He could not become part of government or church or academia. He had to reject their "dead works" in order to "serve the living God."

Only in retrospect did he fully realize what he had done. He later considered his refusal to enter these institutions his *metanoia*, his radical change of mind and heart. Turning his back on the major institutions of the society was for him the beginning of a new life in the spirit. "No social space or field exists outside the powers that be and the existing institutions are all that there is at the moment of one's metanoia, of one's giving up dead works."

"The words make no sense," he later wrote, "the atmosphere is stifled. One chokes. One has no choice but to leave. But one does not know what is going to happen, one has no blueprint for action. The 'decision' literally means . . . being cut off from one's own routines in a paid and honored position. And the trust that this sub-zero situation is bound to create new ways of life is our faith.

"I probably did not advance much in personal virtue by this about-face toward the future, away from any visible institution. I did not become a saint. All I received was life. From then on, I did not have to say anything which did not originate in my heart."

Institutions are good at preserving and passing on the steps humanity has already taken. But they cannot create new life. They cannot lead people into a different future. The Post Office preserves our right to communicate beyond national boundaries, which was originally a revolutionary step. The Post Office preserves that possibility for us, but if you try to get the Post Office to take any radical new steps, you will quickly find that such a massive and established bureaucracy will not easily budge.

People who move beyond the ordinary consciousness and conscience of religious institutions face very much the same problem. They can draw on the words and the symbols for support on their journeys. But they must not expect the institutions to create new life. The community that will support them can only be found along the way, as they themselves take steps into an unknown future.

The traditional spiritual symbols are valid. We must be born again if we are to enter into the kingdom. We must acknowledge our illusions and lies and addictions. We must become part of the people if we are to be saved. We must live by faith and hope and love. We must, somewhere along the way, die to the world that systematically exploits the earth and its creatures. To be saved we must leave deadening power structures and be born again into a new community of life and hope.

People who have moved out of their ordinary existence and committed themselves to critical but shaky enterprises are part of a community still in the making. That community is being formed not around symbols or rituals, but around the life and death issues that the symbols have always pointed to. Symbols can easily be made into realities unto themselves and get enshrined and worshipped as if they were complete. That is why Joseph Campbell insists that myth and symbol are not about something that happened way back then. Rather, they are a key to tell us what we can do now. We have keys to a possible future, but they are useless unless we act on them.

Rabbi Weisenbaum of Tucson, a leader in the Sanctuary movement that protected Central Americans who fled to this country, often told Jews that the most pain they feel in America today is in the dentist's office! The Exodus and the Holocaust, he claimed, are still taking place, but the Salvadorans and Guatemalans have traded places with the Jews. They are the ones standing up to Pharaoh and being persecuted and hunted down because they have taken a stand for justice.

In *Walking the Red Line* Deena Hurwitz introduces us to Israelis who are seeking justice for persecuted Palestinians (New Society Publishers, Philadelphia, PA, 1992). Rabbi Marshal Meyer marched with the women of the *Plaza de Mayo* in Argentina who were protesting the disappearance of their loved ones. He was threatened with death because he dared oppose the Argentine military government. From his roots, he knew that he was standing with the people against Pharaoh. He knew that the symbols exist only to lead us to the radical reality and call of our own time.

Brian Willson lost his legs trying to stop shipments of arms to Nicaragua. The women and children in India chained themselves to the trees so the loggers would not cut the down. Archbishop Romero told the Salvadoran soldiers they should not follow orders to shoot their peasant brothers and sisters. Chico Mendez was killed for trying to save part of the Amazon. Ninez Montenegro Garca risks her life for the families of the disappeared in Guatemala. These are people of extraordinary faith and courage who shake us out of our ordinary existence and face us with the life and death questions of our own moment in history. By entering an existence that does not yet exist, they open out for others the possibility of making changes in their own lives.

History is constantly providing us with opportunities for achieving enlightenment, for moving out of slavery into freedom, for being born again. We are constantly being called into a new existence, out of the lies and devastation and violence all around us. "With every breath of life," wrote Rosenstock-Huessy, "we either start afresh a time that we want to differ from the past, or we continue a time that we want to perpetuate one day more."

To take steps out of the ordinary mainstream existence always means challenging institutional understanding. Years ago, Myles Horton, founder of Highlander Folk School in Tennessee, was talking to Helen Lewis, who had been teaching at a community college in the South and getting her students involved in social action. The college, which wanted nothing to do with social action, dismissed her. She felt bad about herself and talked to Myles about it. "Institutions," Myles mused, "yes, you have to work with them. You have to work with them, but you have to push them. You push them, and they move a little bit. Then you push some more and they may move a little bit farther. Finally you push them until they get to the edge. Then you push once more—and you fall off!"

Among the community of those who have fallen off and the community of those who are still pushing lies the beginning of a different future. And to bring that future into being, we are called to leave the familiar world we have known.

That which gives life to the world is not confined to one place or to one group of people. It does not exist in one nationality or one religion or one economic system or one ideology. Rather, it is continually being called forth from people at the edges of different cultures and religions and nationalities and professions. The Judaeo-Christian symbols can interpret that reality for us and lead us along the way, but no one owns and controls that reality. The Spirit breathes where she will.

We are now at a point in history where massive crisis is breaking in upon us, where people all over the earth are being called to give birth to a different future. They are being called to a new level of consciousness and conscience. They are taking parallel steps on local levels for survival, for peace, and for a sustainable way of living. They are challenging the structures that have been doing violence to the earth and violence to the poor. Some are highly organized; others are simply clusters of individuals trying to live their lives in a responsible fashion. But the questions they are asking and the steps they are taking bring them beyond the group consciousness and conscience of their backgrounds. For the first time in history, we are getting a glimpse of how our actions reverberate around the world, how they affect Gaia, how the future of life on earth hangs in the balance. For the first time, we can see that pledging allegiance to the Whole, not just to a particular nation or corporation or religious institution, is the way of patriotism and piety.

Who, then, will lead us from death into new life if the institutions will not do it? Who will bring us out of the ordinary existence we see all around us, out of the hypocrisy and hopelessness and pollution and hatred and war and weapons and greed? Only those who are listening to the call and making the difficult journey. Those journeys will affect the institutions in time, but institutions seldom lead the way. Eventually, the institutions will benefit by the courage of the few—and will incorporate the values that they once felt so threatened by.

Page Smith, in his *Popular History of the United States*, describes the people who took part in the massive movement for the abolition of slavery in U.S. history. He describes how the movement arose and sub-sided, waxed and waned, and at times almost dropped out of existence. It was fueled by blacks and whites, by women and by runaway slaves, by people from the churches and synagogues, by humanists and by socialists, by artists and writers and politicians. When the gathering of believers reached its peak, and abolition finally became a reality, Page says simply that the "church of the abolition" disbanded.

The community of people who are "called out" gathers itself together again, and again, and again, and is still gathering itself together at this moment. People from every culture and race and nationality are strug-gling and living heroically, fighting for human rights and justice and peace.

These are our brothers and sisters in faith. We do not know them, but we know that they are there. The people of spirit cannot be easily defined; there are no walls of separation, no "ins" and "outs." Whenever people put a fence around themselves and declare themselves a "spiritual people," they have fenced themselves in. They have made it harder to be called anywhere beyond their own enclosures.

The community of those who are called forth will always be acting from the future. They will see a new story and begin to live that story out now, before its time. They will be leaving the old forms behind in order to meet the living God. Jesus told his followers that it was better for them that he go away, because if he stayed, the Spirit could not come to them. The former ways of contact could not be allowed to become idols separat-ing them from the Living God. The name that Yahweh gave himself, "I am who am," can just as correctly be translated "I will be who I will be." If you think you see the Buddha on the road, the saying goes, kill him.

We come to know God only as we enter an unknown future. To make an idol out of that which has already happened is to falsify God. "I will not call God Allah," the novelist Kazantzakis has the dervish say. "A name is a prison and God is free. God is too big to fit inside any name. I will not call God Allah, but AHHH."

The *ekklesia* is always on pilgrimage, always following a vision and a dream. The kingdom will never really come visibly; we will not arrive at a utopia we can see and touch and feel. "Everything good has to be done over and over again forever." Yet there is a community working incessantly to bring the kingdom into being. And we are called to be part of that community of people who are unknown to us but who are following the call into an existence that does not yet exist. For the kingdom is already among us, unrecognized but powerful.

Footnotes

Session Two: The Experience and Dynamics of Violence

[1]Charles McCarthy, "Christian Nonviolence: Option or Obligation?" (Unpublished, transcript of video series, available from AGAPE, 918 North Main Street, Brockton, Mass. 02401), page 6-1.

[2]McCarthy, p. 8-5.

Session Four: Violence, Nonviolence and Gender

[3]*Women in The Front Line: Human Rights Violations Against Women—An Amnesty International Report* (New York Amnesty International Publications, 1990).

[4]See Catherine McKinnon, "Turning Rape into Pornography: Postmodern Genocide," *MS.*, July/August, 1993, pp. 230; Laureen Pitter and Alexander Stiglmayer, "Will the World Remember? Can The World Forget?", *MS*, April/May, 1993, pp. 12-13,19-22.

[5]*Policy on the Criminal Justice System Response to Violence Against Women and Children*, Ministry of Attorney General 1993, p. 2.

[6]See Walsh, Roger. "Toward a Psychology of Sustainability," *Revisions* (Washington: Heldref Publica tions, Fall, 1992), pp. 61-66.

[7]*Family and Sexual Violence, The Facts. B.C. Provincial Report* (Victoria: Queen's Printer, 1992).

[8]Murray A. Strass and Richard J. Gelles. *How Violent Are American Families? Estimates from the National Resurvey and Other Studies*, 1988, p. 26.

[9]Robin Badgley et al. *Sexual Offenses Against Children* (Ottawa: Ministry of Supply and Services, 1984), p.180.

[10]Barbara Appleford. *Family Violence Renew: Prevention and Treatment of Abusive Behavior,* (Ottawa: The Correctional Service of Canada, 1989.

[11]Mcleod, Linda. *Battered But Not Beaten* (Ottawa: Canadian Advisory Council on the Status of Women, 1987).

[12]Adair, Margo. *Working Inside Out: Tools for Change.* (Berkeley: Wingbow Press, 1984).

[13]See "Nonviolence: A Feminist Vision and Strategy," Joanne Sheehan,from *Daring To Change: Perspectives on Feminism and Nonviolence* (War Resister's League: New York), p3.

[14]Bunch, Charlotte. *Going Public With Our Vision* (Denver, CO: Antela Publications, 1985).

[15]Quoted in "Nonviolence: A Feminist Vision and Strategy," by Joanne Sheehan (War Resisters League: New York), p.3.

[16]Ibid.

[17]See "Historical Examples of Nonviolent Struggle", The Albert Einstein Institute, Cambridge, Ma.; "Nonviolence," by Ed Hedemann and *Handbook for Nonviolent Action*, War Resisters League, NY, 1991.

[18]McAllister, Pam. *You Can't Kill The Spirit* (Philadelphia, PA: New Society Publishers, 1989), p.9.

[19]*We Are All Part of One Another: A Barbara Deming Reader*, ed. Jane Meyerding, (Philadelphia, PA: New Society Publishers, 1984), p.290.

[20]Ibid. p.289.

[21]Ibid. p.188.

Session Seven: Nonviolence and Social Transformation

[22] 1994 Human Development Report

[23] Xavier Gorostiaga, S.J., "The New Consensus: A Civilization Based on Harmony and Simplicity," 1995.

[24] Oxfam International, *Multilateral Debt: The Human Costs*, February 1996.

[25] Ibid.

[26] Written by three faith groups: Ecumenical Committee for Corporate Responsibility of the United Kingdom (ECCR); Taskforce on the Churches and Corporate Responsibility of Canada (TCCR) and the Global Accountability Issue Group of the Interfaith Center on Corporate Responsibility (ICCR).

Gunther Anders and Claude Eatherly, *Burning Conscience: The Guilt of Hiroshima* (New York: Paragon House, 1989).

John J. Ansbro, *Martin Luther King, Jr.: The Making of a Mind* (Maryknoll NY: Orbis Books, 1982).

Domingos Barbe, *Theological Roots of Nonviolence* (Las Vegas: Pace e Bene, 1989).

_____, *A Theology of Conflict and Other Writings on Nonviolence* (Maryknoll NY: Orbis, 1989).

Hugo Adam Bedlau, *Civil Disobedience: Theory and Practice* (Indianapolis: Bobbs-Merrill, 1969).

Daniel Berrigan, *To Dwell in Peace* (San Francisco: Harper & Row, 1987).

Kim Bobo, Jackie Kendall, and Steve Max, *A Manual for Activists in the 1990s* (Seven Locks Press, 1991).

Joan Bondurant, *Conquest of Violence* (University of California Press, 1958).

William Borman, *Gandhi and Nonviolence* (Albany NY: State University of New York Press, 1986).

Dom Helder Camara, *The Spiral of Violence* (Sheed and Ward, 1975).

Robert Cooney and Helen Michalowski, *The Power of the People: Active Nonviolence in the United States* (Philadelphia: New Society Publishers, 1987).

Coover, Deacon, Esser and Moore, eds., *Resource Manual for a Living Revolution* (Philadelphia: New Society Publishers 1977).

John Dear, *Disarming the Heart: Toward a Vow of Nonviolence* (New York: Paulist Press, 1987).

_____, *Our God is Nonviolent: Witnesses in the Struggle for Peace and Justice,* (New York: Pilgrim Press, 1990).

_____, *The God of Peace: Toward a Theology of Nonviolence* (Maryknoll, NY: Orbis Books, 1994).

_____, *Seeds of Non-Violence* (Baltimore: Fortkamp Publishing Co., 1992).

Barbara Deming, *We Cannot Live Without Our Lives* (Grossman Publishers, 1974).

_____, *Revolution and Equilibrium* (Grossman Publishers, 1971).

Narayan Desai, *Toward a Nonviolent Revolution* (Sarva Seva Sangh Prakashan).

James W. Douglass, *Lightning East to West* (New York: Crossroad, 1983).

_____, *The Nonviolent Coming of God* (Maryknoll NY: Orbis, 1991).

_____, *The Nonviolent Cross: A Theology of Revolution and Peace* (New York: Macmillan, 1966).

_____, *Resistance and Contemplation* (Garden City NY: Doubleday, 1972).

Erik Erickson, *Gandhi's Truth* (New York: W.W. Norton, 1969).

Louis Fischer, *The Life of Mahatma Gandhi,* (New York: Harper & Row, 1954).

Erich Fromm, *The Anatomy of Human Destructiveness* (Holt).

M.K. Gandhi, *My Experiments with Truth* [also published as *Gandhi: An Autobiography*] (Boston: Beacon Press, 1957).

_____, *Nonviolence in Peace and War* (New York: Garland Press, 1972).

_____, *Nonviolent Resistance* (Schoken Books, 1962).

_____, *Pathway to God* (Ahmedabad, India: Navajivan Publishing House).

_____, *Satyagraha in South Africa* (New York, 1954).

_____, K. Kripalani, ed., *All Men Are Brothers: Autobiographical Reflections* (New York, Continuum, 1980).

The Garland Library of War and Peace (New York: Garland Publishing Inc., 1970). A collection of 360 titles reprinted in 328 volumes.

Richard Gregg, *The Power of Nonviolence* (London: James Clark, 1960 and Schoken Books, 1970).

A. Paul Hare and Herbert H. Blumberg, eds., *Nonviolent Direct Action* (Washington and Cleveland: Corpus Books, 1968).

Vincent Harding, *Hope and History: Why We Must Share the Story of the Movement* (Maryknoll, NY: Orbis Books, 1990).

Bernard Haring, *The Healing Power of Peace and Nonviolence* (Paulist Press, 1986).

Robert L. Holmes, *Nonviolence in Theory and Practice* (Belmont CA: Wadsworth, 1990).

Johan Holst, *Civilian-Based Defense in a New Era* (Boston: Albert Einstein Institution for Nonviolent Sanctions, 1990).

Gerard Houver, *A Nonviolent Lifestyle: Conversations with Jean and Hildegard Goss-Mayr* (1981).

Catherine Ingram, *In the Footsteps of Gandhi: Conversations with Spiritual Social Activists* (Parallax Press, 1990).

Narayan Jayaprakash, *Total Revolution* (Sarva Seva Sangh Prakashan, 1975).

Ignatius Jesudasan, *A Gandhian Theology of Liberation* (Maryknoll, NY: Orbis Books, 1984).

M.L. King, Jr., *Loving Your Enemies* [pamphlet], M.L. King, Jr., A.J. Muste Foundation, n.d.

_____, *Strive Toward Freedom* (Harper & Row, 1958).

_____, *Trumpet of Conscience* (New York: Harper & Row, 1967).

_____, *Why We Can't Wait* (Harper and Row, 1964).

Mary Lou Kownacki and Gerard Vanderhaar, *Way of Peace: A Guide to Nonviolence* (Pax Christi, 1987).

George Lakey et al., *Powerful Peacemaking: A Strategy for a Living Revolution* (New Society Publishers, 1987).

Arthur J. Laffin and Anne Montgomery, *Swords into Plowshares* (San Francisco: Harper & Row, 1987).

Staughton Lynd, ed., *Nonviolence in America* (Bobbs-Merrill Co., 1966).

Pam McAllister, ed., *Reweaving the Web of Life: Feminism and Nonviolence* (Philadelphia: New Society Publishers, 1982).

_____, *You Can't Kill the Spirit: Stories of Women and Nonviolent Action* (Philadelphia: New Society Publishers, 1991).

G.H.C. Macgregor, *The New Testament Basis of Pacifism* (Nyack NY: Fellowship Publications, 1936).

J. Massyngbaerde Ford, *My Enemy is My Guest: Jesus and Violence in Luke* (Maryknoll NY: Orbis Books, 1984).

Philip McManus and Gerald Schlabach, eds., *Relentless Persistence: Nonviolent Action in Latin America* (Philadelphia: New Society Publishers, 1991).

Thomas Merton, *Faith and Violence* (South Bend: Notre Dame Press, 1968).

Ched Myers, *Binding the Strong Man: A Political Reading of Mark's Story of Jesus* (Maryknoll NY: Orbis Books, 1988).

Michael Nagler, *America Without Violence: Why Violence Persists and How You Can Stop It* (Covelo, CA: Island Press, 1982).

Angie O'Gorman, ed., *The Universe Bends Toward Justice: A Reader on Christian Nonviolence* (Philadelphia: New Society Publishers, 1991).

Roger S. Powers and William B. Vogele, eds., *Protest, Power, and Change: An Encyclopedia of Nonviolent Action from ACT-UP to Women's Suffrage* (New York, London: Garland Publishing Co, 1997).

Fred Ross, *Conquering Goliath: Cesar Chavez at the Beginning* (Keen, CA).

Mark Shepard, *Gandhi Today* (Seven Locks Press, 1981).

Gene Sharp, *Gandhi as a Political Strategist* (Boston: Porter Sargent, 1979).

_____, *The Politics of Nonviolent Action*. Three volumes. (Boston: Porter Sargent, 1973).

Leo Tolstoi, *Writings On Civil Disobedience and Nonviolence* (Philadelphia: New Society Publishers, 1987).

Andre Trocme, *Jesus and the Nonviolent Revolution* (Scottsdale, PA: Herald Press, 1973).

Michael True, *Justice Seekers, Peace Makers: 32 Portraits in Courage* (Mystic CT: Twenty-third Publications, 1987).

Gerard A. Vanderhaar, *Enemies and How to Love* Them (Twenty-Third Publications, 1985).

_____, *Nonviolence in Christian Tradition* (Pax Christi: 1983).

_____, *Nonviolence Theory and Practice* (Mid-South Peace and Justice Center, 1985).

James Washington, *A Testament of Hope: The essential Writings and Speeches of Martin Luther King, Jr.* (Hayes-Collins, 1986).

Sharon Welch, *Communities of Resistance and Solidarity: A Feminist Theology of Liberation* (Maryknoll, NY: Orbis Books, 1985).

Walter Wink, *Engaging the Powers: Discernment and Resistance in a World of Domination* (Minneapolis: Fortress, 1992).

_____, *Violence and Nonviolence in South Africa: Jesus' Third Way* (Philadelphia: New Society Publishers, 1987).

J.H. Yoder, *The Politics of Jesus* (Grand Rapids MI: Wm. B. Eerdmans, 1972).

Franklin Zahn, *Deserter from Violence: Experiments with Gandhi's Truth* (New York: Philosophical Library, 1984).

Gordon Zahn, *In Solitary Witness: The Life and Death of Franz Jaggerstatter* (Philadelphia: Templegate, 1986).